I DON'T WANT TO COMPLAIN,

BUT...

*Teen Conversations
with God*

by Ted Schroeder

CONCORDIA
PUBLISHING HOUSE

For Kristen, my collaborator
for Ted and Naomi, my truth-tellers
and for Ellen, my support

Copyright © 1985 by Concordia Publishing House
3558 S. Jefferson Ave., St. Louis, MO 63118-3968
Manufactured in the United States of America

Library of Congress Cataloging in Publication Data

Schroeder, Theodore W., 1939-
    I don't want to complain, but—

    1. Youth—Prayer-books and devotions—English.
I. Title.
BV4531.2.S375 1985   242'.63   84-22989
ISBN 0-570-03964-9

4 5 6 7 8 9 10   94 93

I Don't Want to Complain, but . . .

CONTENTS

Lord, I don't want to complain, but I'd like to tell you about . . .

Foreword

FOREWORD

What Is This Book About?

In a recent *Peanuts* cartoon, Charlie Brown observes that life "has its ups and downs." To which Lucy responds with something like, "Why does life have downs? I don't want any downs! Just ups! More and more ups!"

She has a point. It would be great if life could be a series of ups and all the downs would disappear. But that will not happen, at least not in this life.

Emotionally, we are always on the way up or down. And often, especially in our teen years, the trips from up to down can happen pretty fast and furiously. It doesn't take long to get from riding high to going down into the pits. And sometimes the pits are pretty grim.

And what do we do when we are in the pits? Cry? Complain? Feel sorry for ourselves? Probably.

But one thing the children of God through the ages have done is to "tell" Him about the problem and ask His help. "Prayers" that present our troubles to God sound a lot like complaints. But He promises to hear and help, even when we complain.

Scripture is full of these kinds of "complaints"—of personal "prayers" that bring to God the hurt and helplessness of one of His children. You might read some of them in Psalm 32, 55, or 109, for example; or in Jer. 15:15-18 or 20:7-13. Some of these prayers are restated in modern speech throughout this book for you.

Our Lord is not impatient with our complaints. He is not too busy to hear us when we bring any problem to Him. He understands when we come up against things in life that send us into the pits and make us wonder if we will ever get out again, ever smile again, ever look forward to tomorrow again.

Perhaps, sometimes we are reluctant to take our hurts to Jesus. We think they are too unimportant or that we shouldn't be bothering Him with little problems. We think that we ought to be able to handle things on our own, and that somehow we'll be able to pull ourselves out of the pits.

But He invites us to speak to Him—in whatever words are in our hearts. And He promises to hear us when we pray—even when we complain about our hurts and problems. And Jesus promises to stay with us, to help us and to renew us by the power of the Spirit.

So this book invites you to complain—not in a selfish, "poor me" kind of a way. But in the way one of my teens sometimes comes to us with a problem that is bothering her. It might be something around the house she'd like changed, or something she'd like us to handle more fairly. And she says, "Mom and Dad, not to be ignorant, but . . ." And she explains the problem from her point of view.

In that spirit—in the spirit of telling our Lord our troubles and asking for His help. In the spirit of the Savior Himself, who came to God one night with His complaint—"If it be possible, let this cup pass from Me. But not My will, but Yours be done"—in that spirit we encourage you, child of God, to approach your loving Savior, who seeks to help you in whatever pit of trouble or hurt you find yourself.

How You Can Use This Book

The "conversations" in this book are "complaints" as young people might tell them to a special Friend. Perhaps some of the problems, some of the concerns are those that have brought you down as well.

Jesus offered many words of comfort during His lifetime. Often those started with phrases like, "Don't be afraid"; "My peace I give You"; "Come to Me" and many more. He is "Savior and Friend" not only when things are going good, but also when we hurt or are troubled or when we are caught in a problem we cannot solve. A wise person once said that "true prayer is bringing the problem to Jesus and leaving it with Him."

Use these words (or your own) to bring your "complaints" to our Lord, who has promised to hear and help. Surely the problems and concerns raised by these conversations are not easily solved. For example, we do not completely understand the will of God, develop a healthy self-image, or overcome jealousy by one conversation with the Savior. But we are promised further "enlightenment" and growth when we study His Word. As we open ourselves to the work of the Spirit through the Word, we are strenghtened in our faith, led to answers to our questions, and shown ways to break through our confusion. For that reason you will find a section at the back of this book that offers suggestions to help you dig into the Word. These Bible-study activities are intended to guide you as you think more deeply about the questions raised by these conversations. After each section of this book, you will find several letters listed under a heading "Ask . . . Seek . . . Knock." These letters correspond with suggestions for study under that heading at the back of the book. You are encouraged to use one or more of these to lead you into the Word.

Jesus promised that our study will be blessed. He told us that when we "ask" it will be given to us, when we "seek" we will "find," and when we "knock" it will be "opened" to us. Use these Bible-study exercises to fill yourself with His Word so that as you communicate with Him the promise of His strength and forgiveness will help you out of the pits of doubt and confusion and back to the place where life smiles, and you find once again the joy of life in Him— the joy He wants you to have.

TESTS AND MORE TESTS

Lord Jesus,

I am so happy. For the first time in months I could just flip. This time, for the first time, I did it—or we did it. This time turning my brain into a stone studying did some good.

Finally I got an A on a chemistry test.

Every other time the words and the numbers and the symbols all wanted to stay in a stupid jumble in my head, and the test looked like it was written in Arabic or something.

But this this time something worked right.

I almost panicked when I saw the essay questions. Can you believe that guy, putting essay questions on a chemistry test? He must sit up nights thinking of ways to wipe out his students. And when I talk to him about it, he just gives me that silly grin and says, "Just do your best."

I'd like to give him a test.

Anyway, I wrote something down. It must have been all right because there it was—a big scrawly, beautiful A right on my paper.

Thanks for hearing me and helping me.

9

But, you know what's best about this whole thing—the part that really makes me want to sing in the halls and walk on the walls is that weird old Marcia got a C, believe it or not.

I know she did. I saw that C as plain as day, just before she turned her test over and started to drop tears all over the back page.

Every other time we get a test back she leans over and wiggles her head in that "aren't-I-great-and-aren't-I-lucky-to-be-me" way and says, "What'd ya get?"

I'd like to tell her that it's none of her stupid business what I got, but I usually end up muttering something about not as good as last time—or something else.

"Well," she says, looking down her snooty nose, "I got my (usual) A."

She doesn't really say usual, but she might as well. And then she laughs that queer little giggle of hers and waves her paper around for everyone to see. It's enough to make you sick. You'd think her papers would catch fire the way I look at them.

Today I couldn't help it. I just leaned over to weepy Marcia and said, "Well, Marcia, old friend, how'd ya do on this little gem?" And I flopped my paper around a little under her drippy nose.

She didn't answer me. Just blubbered something about a bad day.

"Too bad, Marcia. Maybe next time," I go.

Now I KNOW I should not have done that. I thought I would feel great after giving Marcia a little of her own medicine. But I didn't. I felt crummy.

I guess it's not Marcia's papers I hate. It's her. I guess I hate Marcia when she shows off and shows me up.

Everything comes easy for Marcia. I don't think she even studies. She just waltzes in to the room and aces every test. Well, almost every test.

But see, that's just it. I don't want to hate her. I don't want to hate anybody. I don't want to feel good just because someone else is feeling bad.

Can You help me?

I'm sorry for how I feel about Marcia and the others who get A's and never even try. I'm sorry for the times I get angry at You when I think You short-changed me in the brains department.

I know You made me the way I am and it's for the best for me, even though there are a few things I'd like to change. I know you made Marcia the way she is, and that I have as good a chance of making something out of my life as she does—maybe better.

Forgive me for my hates, my bad feelings, and the time I spend feeling sorry for myself. And help me be happy just for me when I get A's—and content because I did my best when I get C's. We might even work on being happy for old Marcia and her show-off papers.

It won't be easy, but I know You will help me because You love me.

Thanks.

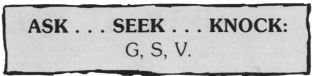

ASK . . . SEEK . . . KNOCK:
G, S, V.

2

MOM'S UPTIGHT AGAIN

Lord Jesus,

I wish she could just relax. Why is everything such a big deal? Mom's always rattled, always flying about four feet off the ground, and most of the time she lands right on me. Company's coming and she's off into space. Or company's not coming and she's having a fit.

Time to get ready!

Time to go!

Time to clean!

Time to get the dishes done!

"We have to get at that basement," she goes.

"Clean your closet and drawers. When I was a little girl I had to clean mine every week. And I'll bet you haven't touched yours in months."

Right, Mom. But what's the problem? They're my drawers and it's my closet.

The other Saturday I counted. She had eight things for me to do before I even got out of my pajamas. And by the time I had my hair fixed it was eight more. And then she was surprised when I freaked out and yelled at her. What does she expect?

I can't even remember eight jobs, let alone get them all done.

I always feel so sorry after I yell at her. I know you're not supposed to yell at your mom. Even when I don't remember, she reminds me, and my dad reminds me, and my friends remind me, and You remind me.

I don't want to be that way. I'd like to hear everything she's got to say and smile that little girl smile she likes to see, and do all the jobs with the hustle in my bustle she expects.

But I can't. Why can't she understand that I'm a person too? I deserve to be treated like someone who counts for something. What I want to do—my plans are important to me too. Is that too much to ask?

What I'd really like to ask You is to change her (even though I know it can't be). But wouldn't it be nice if she could be different? In an instant, like magic she might be less . . . less, I don't know—rattled, I guess.

Sometimes I dream of what life might be like if she was all laid back like an algebra teacher.

In this unbelievably cool voice, she'd say, "We have company coming in three hours and forty-seven minutes. I believe we might take a moment or two to formulate a plan that will ready us and the house for their arrival. Of course our plan will have to include some improvement in the state of your room and your personal attire, but I don't see why that can't be accomplished rather easily in the time we have."

But that wouldn't be her. "For the last time, get your room cleaned up and get some decent clothes on right this minute!" sounds more like Mom.

Suzy says, "At least be glad you have a mom to yell at you."

That doesn't really help much when she's on my case. But I know what Suzy's saying. Behind all the scolding and nagging, one thing's for sure. She loves me. She may not always show it, at least not the way I'd like her to. But every word, every push and pull is supposed to be for my good. She wouldn't even know how to act any other way.

Forgive me for the angry words and the bad feelings. I'd like to take them all back if I could. But maybe it will be just as good if You take them all away.

And help me love her. Even when she's all mouth and

13

"hurry up." When she's into her do-this-now-and-don't-do-that-then routine?

Help me see past the words and worry, the frantics and the frazzle to that place in her that is permanent, for sure love for me—no matter what.

Like the way You love me.

And help me love her back.

Thanks.

ASK . . . SEEK . . . KNOCK:
P, R, Y.

3

THE SAINT

Lord Jesus,

This is not a real big deal or anything. But I can't help wondering sometimes about Norma. I know the other kids think she's a complete jerk. And I have to admit that she definitely is a little weird. But yesterday we sat together in study hall, and we talked. She didn't seem that strange. I mean she talked about her folks, and her brother, and what she was gonna do this summer, all like that. Just like any normal person.

Later in the hall, Sally says to me, she goes, "Look out now, we just might hear a hymn or two." I guess she thought that was funny.

But that's just it about Norma. She is so religious. I mean, she carries a Bible with her at all times. It's almost like a part of her arm, or something. And she holds her head up real straight and doesn't talk much to anyone. You see her sitting by herself a lot and about the only time she talks in class is when she thinks something is wrong. Like that time she jumped all over Alvin when he said that dumb stuff about showing R rated movies in assembly. She got real excited about that and preached a little sermon about how bad the movies are. I was pretty impressed **15** with all the Bible passages she knew right there on the tip of her tongue. The other kids just made fun.

I guess they mostly make fun of Norma. They call her a Psalm-singer or Goody-Goody (G.G. for short). But old Norma is tough, you gotta give her that. She just pokes that pointy nose of hers right up in the air and breezes past like she does't hear a word.

But what I wonder about is if Norma is really doing what You want her to do. Is she being the kind of follower You want? Should I be more like Norma, all religious and quiet, reading my Bible in lunch hall and yelling about all the bad stuff people do?

I try to picture myself doing that. I think about what it would be like to be Norma. And I think about what I would do if they started calling me names and laughing. I'd probably kick somebody. Especially that jerk Vince. If he said a word I'd punch a hole in his head and let all the air out.

But anyway, I just don't think I'd make it as Norma. I mean, I guess she's got a point about reading the Bible and all—and there sure is enough bad stuff going on, even at our school that you might come down on. But I wonder. Is that what You really have in mind?

The other night I thought about what You might do if You came to our school. I suppose You'd shake Your head a lot at first. Or maybe You'd cry, I don't know.

But I just don't think You'd sit around with good old Norma in a corner somewhere reading the Bible and praying. Anyway, that's not what You did the first time, is it?

And I don't think You'd call an assembly and yell at everyone about how bad they are either. I mean, most people know all of that. Maybe that's why they feel so bad when Norma's around. I know she makes me feel ashamed a lot of times.

But I think You would help. I think You'd listen to Sarah when she wants to run away from home again. And You'd sit with Paul when he talks about killing himself. And I think You'd probably try to do something for the burnouts who don't even seem to be in class when they're there.

I think You'd just love people and try to help out, the way You did. At least that is the way it seems to me.

I guess I'd like to be more like that myself.

Oh, I know I got a long way to go. I spend a lot of time

worrying about getting my sleep, about my parties, my friends, my games and all that other "my" stuff that is on my brain all the time.

But I like it when I can help. And it seems like someone is always crying.

Lord Jesus, can You help me be a little more like You might be if You walked around the halls and sat around in the lunch room with the kids?

I'd like that.

And I guess we'd better just leave Norma's way of doing things to Norma. Maybe You could help her too. I think she's afraid.

Thanks.

ASK . . . SEEK . . . KNOCK:
J, T, Z.

THE MIRROR

Lord Jesus,

Well, I guess this is it. This is what I've got to work with. The old beak is still there, the zits and the squinty eyes. I keep waiting for an attack of macho man to come over me and to see Robert Redford or somebody peering back at me when I get set to hack at my eighteen whiskers in the morning, but so far—nothing.

Mom says, "Don't be silly. You're not ugly. Just . . . Well, let's say you're special."

Nice try, Mom. An alligator is special too, but I don't think I'd like to look like one.

I guess I'd really like to ask You for a small miracle. Not that I need to look like a movie star or anything. But if You could just make me so that the girls might be interested and not turn away. It wouldn't take a whole lot. Just a little rearranging of what's there anyway.

Funny. I know a lot of kids who'd like to change their looks. Some of them are pretty sharp looking. At least I think so. But they're not happy with this or that—eyes too close or chin too pointy, stuff like that.

You know what You should have done. You should have left everyone's face like modeling clay. Then when they wanted to look a different way, they could just work around on it for a while and come up with something better.

But I suppose that wouldn't work. I mean, how would it be to have everyone look like whoever was popular in the movies or on videos? There's probably enough of that just with clothes.

And Mom says, "Be happy you're not really ugly."

I'm not sure if that means I'm just a little ugly or that really ugly people don't have to ask. But anyway.

I guess we make too much out of faces. I mean, the nicest guy I know looks like his face was put together in our chemistry lab. And this girl Lois. She's fun to be with and I like her. But she looks like a linebacker.

Funny about faces. People think they know you from your face. They think that pretty faces make pretty people. Maybe they don't really think that, because everyone who has lived more than two weeks knows that isn't true. But everyone acts that way.

Can You help me feel better about my face—and the rest of me too, for that matter? I'm not saying I wouldn't change if I could, but I might as well get used to me. Whenever I take a peek in a mirror, this is the pan that is going to stare back at me. I might as well get to like it as much as I can.

I'm sorry for the times I feel sorry for myself and angry at You because I am not made the way I think I should be. Help me with that and forgive me.

Sometimes I wonder if You were really as pretty as the Sunday school pictures make You out to be. I think maybe You weren't. Maybe You were just a plain kind of a guy that no one paid much attention to until You talked. Maybe that was one of the reasons not very many followed You.

In any case, I could use Your help with this. I want to be happier with myself, face and all. I know You will help me because You love me—whatever I look like. And that's good to know.

And maybe You could help someone else who is special to see past my beak and squinty eyes, and love me too.

I'd like that.

Thanks.

ASK . . . SEEK . . . KNOCK:
A, F, N.

5

ZITS AND MOSQUITOES

Lord Jesus,

You know Ralph, that brainy kid in psychology class who is always throwing around these forty-dollar words and arguing about everything. I guess he's studying to be an atheist. He's always talking about "counterevidences for God."

For him its some kind of a big deal that children are starving in Africa and that a lot of innocent people die in wars and like that. He says he doesn't see how a loving God could let that kind of thing happen.

I guess he has a point. I mean, nobody likes to see children starving or people dying in wars. But I'm not so sure that's all Your fault. Seems to me that children starve because whoever has their food is not giving it to them, and people who shoot other people in a war don't always get Your permission first. But Ralph is real mad about all of that. I guess it's good that he's mad, anyway. Maybe he can do something, even if he doesn't always believe that You are there and that You care.

Sometimes I have trouble believing too. But it's not starving children that get to me. For me it's zits. How can You really care about me when what happened last week happened? I didn't

21

think that Paul would ever ask me for a date. I mean, he hardly ever even said anything to me. But all of a sudden, he really came through. And I was so happy. I felt like I had been chosen prom queen and court all rolled into one. And then . . . Well, You know what happened. There, right on the end of my nose this huge zit just appeared.

I looked like Rudolph. I tried to cover it with makeup, but the more makeup I put on the more my nose looked like a painted banana in the center of my face.

And about the first thing bright-boy Paul says is, "Is something wrong with your nose?"

See? How could You let that happen? I looked forward to that date for so long and I spent the whole night feeling just miserable.

It was like the time we went camping last year. You know how we spent a lot of nights in crummy campgrounds that seemed to be filled with nothing but rowdy kids and garbage cans. But then we got to that place that was just perfect. I mean, the little lake was like a mirror and there was hardly a soul around for miles. We made that little campfire and Dad finally relaxed enough to start to enjoy himself. And the sun slowly slipped away to a golden glow—like they say. And all of a sudden it sounded like the insect air force was moving in formation out of the woods. I have never, ever seen that many mosquitoes in one place in my life.

We tried to sit out for a while, smacked at the bugs and tried to talk. But it just didn't work and we ended up trying to play cards by lantern in the tent. It was so hot. And the mosquitoes got in there too. So much batting and bleeding went on in that we thought we might have to send for the Red Cross.

See? Something good and it was spoiled. Does it always have to be that way?

What good are zits and mosquitoes? Are they there just to bug us and make us miserable? Why? Why do we need to be miserable? Isn't life miserable enough without creating things just to make it harder?

I could love You better if I could understand. I don't want explanations for all those hairy questions that seem to get to old Ralph—why You made the world and why there is evil. I don't even want to blame You for starving children or war. But I sure would like to know why, if You love me, You bothered to make zits and mosquitoes.

Can You help me? I don't want to doubt You or Your love for me. I don't want to question You or act like I'm so smart. But I don't understand.

I guess I'm afraid it will always be that way—that every good time will be ruined by some kind of a zit, some kind of a mosquito that will take all the laughter away and leave us sad again. And I so much would like my life to be happy.

Forgive me for these dumb questions. I know they must not seem very important to You.

I guess the best part is to know that You do care enough to listen, even if the zits and mosquitoes are still going to be there.

I keep seeing You sitting with Peter on the beach that time after Peter had denied You. You didn't yell at Peter, or scold him or anything. You just said, "Peter, do you love Me?" I guess You were asking Peter if he had anything he wanted to talk about, anything he needed help with.

I know You hear me and love me. I know that because of what You did for me. But I can't help wondering sometimes. I know You understand.

I guess the happy times without anything to spoil them don't happen much in this life. Maybe that's part of what's so special about heaven.

But in the meantime, help me to find happiness in spite of zits and mosquitoes and undependable friends, rainy days, and all that other stuff that tries to send every day into the pits.

Help me laugh. I think You'd like me to. There's enough sadness in the world. Even old Ralph knows that.

Thanks for being there, and for caring.

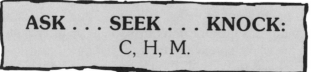

ASK . . . SEEK . . . KNOCK:
C, H, M.

OLD PEOPLE

Lord Jesus,

I know there is going to be another yelling match. This is the day that Mom says we have to go to the home to visit Uncle Frank.

I hate visiting Uncle Frank.

I don't care what anyone says, that home where they got him stinks. I mean it literally stinks. It smells like an uncleaned bathroom. And all those old people sitting around, some of them crying and grabbing at you. It grosses me out. I can hardly stand it.

"Hey, girlie, come over by me," the old men go.

And Uncle Frank grabs onto my hand and I can hardly get him to let go.

And he's so deaf. I don't think he hears more than three words the whole time we're there.

He looks so bad. All shrunk up and wrinkled. He breaths with his mouth open and his skin is like tissue paper—you can see the outline of his bones and all his veins. It's too much.

And Mom is always after me to go with her when she visits. "You should be glad to visit and bring a little joy to the old people there," she goes. "How can you be so selfish? Surely your uncle, who used to give you all those gifts, deserves a little of your time and attention."

And the worst part about it all is that she is right. I should want to go. I should want to try to bring some joy or whatever to Uncle Frank and all those other poor old people in that home. I should be lining up my friends to go along with me and spending a couple hours over there and should make the rounds and talk to all the grabby old men and comb hair for all the silly-talking old women.

But I can't do it. I get depressed just thinking about it. I feel like I'm trapped when I'm in there. I feel like I'm gonna faint or throw up or something.

I don't know why. Maybe it's just too sad. Maybe I feel so sorry for those people who sit there for hours every day, the ones who cry like babies, the ones who can't even hold their heads up any more—I just can't stand it.

Maybe I see in them a picture of myself some day, and it's too scary even to think about. Is that it? Am I just afraid to face the fact that my mom and dad will get old and sit in a chair like that, and I will get old and smell of urine and look at people with eyes that don't really see anymore?

"You've got to be strong for their sake," says Mom.

Right, Mom. You are so exactly right. I've got to be stronger and better able to cope with things like that. I've got to stop thinking about myself and start thinking about what the others are feeling.

Lord Jesus, I need You to help me. This is so hard for me. How do I help being grossed out by sick and sad things like old people and the homes they keep them in? How do I keep from running away?

I wonder if You ever felt like running away. I suppose You did. Maybe that's what You were talking about when You prayed in the Garden. Maybe You understand how I feel. I'd like to think that You do.

And help my Mom understand too. I don't hate Uncle Frank. I love what he used to be. I love how he used to laugh and call me Snicklefritz and bring me toys. But that empty shell of a person in the home doesn't seem like Uncle Frank to me. It's just an old person who holds too tight to my hand.

25

I'll go again to the home today. And I'll try to smile. And I'll try to keep from getting sick. And I'll try to think of them instead of me.

But I'll need Your help and forgiveness too. I don't think I'll ever be able to do it with the kind of joy I'm supposed to have. I don't think I'll ever be able to do it without wanting to run away.

Help me try.

Thanks.

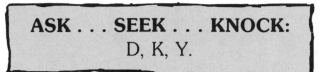

ASK . . . SEEK . . . KNOCK:
D, K, Y.

SUNDAY MORNING

Lord Jesus,

You know, all in all it's pretty comfortable sitting here. Not that the pew is that great, but the music is as familiar as the faces and everyone acts like they could do this in their sleep. Or maybe they do, I don't know.

Like the Franklins over there. The two of them always sit in the same place. And she is always wearing the same face. She looks like a drivers examination officer with an ulcer. And I think the poor guy must work nights, or something, because he just can't stay awake. I mean, he tries all right. He bites his lip and shifts around, and looks at his watch. But he always nods off. And she whacks him with her elbow and he jumps. It's all just part of what we do on Sundays.

Some kids really fight going to church. I suppose its not too cool if you are into trying to prove something. And as Mike says, "It sure is boring."

I guess it depends on what you're looking for. Compared to a rock concert this probably falls off the bottom of the chart. But rock concerts are pretty crowded and usually give me a headache.

If you don't fight it, this isn't so bad. There's lots of stuff to look at and wonder about. Like that very strange wall statue over there. Three people standing together. I guess one of them is supposed to be You. But even when I look at it up close I can't make out who the others are or even who they are supposed to be. You'd be surprised how much time you can spend wondering about something like that. The greatest puzzle for me is why whoever put it up there decided to do it. I mean, what was he trying to say? It must have been something.

And Pastor Sheffield is okay for an older guy. You gotta admit he puts a lot of himself into what he does on Sunday. Not that he is any kind of a threat to Billy Graham. But you sure wouldn't call him laid back. He even has a special way of talking that he saves for church. I mean any other time when he talks about You he says God, just like anybody else. But when he's up there in front he goes—I don't know. It sounds like Gawd, or something like that. I'm not sure why he does that. Maybe it is supposed to make everything seem more important.

And he kinda bounces around when he preaches. You can always tell when he is coming to something important, because he gets up on his toes almost like a dancer.

Mom likes it, but I think he yells too much. He could say the whole thing a lot quieter and everyone could still hear just fine. But maybe he's afraid Mr. Franklin's problem might get to be an epidemic and there is enough elbow whacking going on already.

But sometimes I wonder what You think about all this. Is this what You had in mind when You told us to worship You?

It sure is all very proper. It's like a big, slow dance—every step comes just at the right time in the right place. Is that what You want?

And the people show up. At least a lot of them do. But they don't do much, at least they don't seem to put much of themselves into what they do. They stand and read and sing and listen. Is that what You want?

And the prayers. They for sure cover everything. We pray for every person and for the government and people in trouble and all like that. And I suppose that is a good thing to do, but Mr. Franklin once fell asleep standing there and Mrs. Franklin missed him with her elbow as he slumped over. Is that what You want?

Well, anyway. Even though I complain about it at home, I guess there is nothing I'd be able to do about it, even if people would listen to me.

Whatever I'd say people would probably just keep on doing things the same way. Because they're used to it and it's comfortable—just like it is for me.

Can You help me hear You better in spite of Mr. Franklin and the too long prayers and too slow hymns? Can you help me find You in Pastor Sheffield's tiptoe words and in all the rest of our safe and same Sunday routine?

I'd like to be able to.

Help me know that You are here with me—not because of what we do, but because You love me. Help me remember that what is important is not how well we do with coming to You, but that we come together to worship You, and help and encourage one another as we do.

For all the wondering about it, I can see that You are in the center of that wall statue. I suppose that's why it's there. Forgive me for my wandering and wondering and help me to see You in the middle of everything we do. That's probably what it's all for anyway.

Happy Sunday!

And by the way, maybe You could do something for poor Mr. Franklin. Maybe help him get on the day shift?

Thanks.

ASK . . . SEEK . . . KNOCK:
B, G, Z.

MY OWN
SET OF KEYS

Lord Jesus,

It's not that I love keys so much. They make lumps in your pockets and you can never find them when you need them. But I may go nuts if I don't get my own set of keys for the car.

Dad thinks that every time he gives me the keys he has to give me a little talk at the same time.

Like Saturday. Mike and this guy Roger were over and we were just messing around. We decided to go bowl a couple of games. Mike had his car, but it wasn't running too good. So I thought we could take our car. But I had to ask Dad for the keys.

Believe it or not, as he stood up to get the keys out of his pocket he started in on this favorite lecture of his about the adult responsibilities of using an automobile, as he calls it.

I couldn't believe my ears. There I stood with my hand out, right in front of my friends, and he is going on about how it's important to drive "defensively" or whatever. And then, with the keys tight in his fist, he goes on to tell this story about what happened to some kid in his high school who decided to show off for his friends and ended up racing a train, or some weird thing like that.

I told Dad that I didn't plan to race any trains.

But he does it to me every time. I think he thinks he's helping me. That somehow saying those words before I get in the car is going to make me a better driver, or more careful, or whatever. I guess he wants me to take the whole thing very seriously. He's always going on about this family or that who are insurance poor because their kids had too many accidents and their rates are— "out of this world" is the way he says it.

But what bugs me is that he really doesn't trust me. He ought to know by now that I am not some jerk who gets his kicks from doing a cheap imitation of the "Dukes of Hazzard" or anything like that.

I have never even put a dent in the car. And still I get the lecture. It's like Dad expects me to do something dumb just because I'm a teenager.

I guess it must be scary for him, and he doesn't know how else to show it. He can't ride along with me, so he sends some good advice. I guess he figures it can't hurt.

But it does hurt. It hurts me, especially when he does it in front of my friends. It makes him look like a turkey and me look like a wimp.

Can You help me? I need Your help to deal with this. It'd be pretty hard for Dad to change. I know that. Not only does he think he is helping, he probably is afraid for me and doesn't know what to do about it.

I need Your help to talk to him about it. The talking part is not so hard. It's the talking without getting mad—without yelling—where we need help. Help me be more patient and listen to him instead of just getting mad at him.

And help me understand his fears. The easy thing for me to do would be to ignore him, treat him badly, try to get back. But none of that will do any good. Help me do things in a way that will help him trust me more.

Maybe then, even if he won't get me my own set of keys, **31**

I can get his keys without a "Remember This When You Drive"
pep talk.
    I'd like that.
    Thanks.

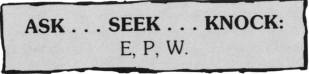

ASK . . . SEEK . . . KNOCK:
E, P, W.

LOOKING
UNDER MY BED

Lord Jesus,

I know You know this already, but maybe telling You about it will help. Every night, just before I get in bed, I have to get down on all fours and look under my bed. If I don't, I just can't get to sleep.

I'm not sure what I think I'll find under there. In fact, if I did find anything I'd probably scream so loud they'd think the tornado siren went off. But if I don't look, it just bugs me until I have to get up, turn on the light, and look.

The other night, you know, when Mom popped in just as I was looking. I don't know what she thought. I don't know if she believed that I had to look for my tennis shoes in the middle of the night before I could go to sleep. But that sounded better than telling her the truth. What should I have said?

"Mom, I know I'm a big girl now and that I will soon drive a car and often go places on my own. I know that in a couple of years I will probably be living in my own place. But still, before I can go to sleep at night, I have to make sure there are no dead bodies or strange people hiding under my bed, even though I know there is not enough room under there for either."

33

Sounds great, right?

Maybe I'm a little weird or whacko or something. Do other people do that?

And what if I get married? Will I still have to look?

"What are you doing there, Hon?" he'll go from the bed.

"Oh, I'm just checking for dead bodies," I'll say.

The marriage will probably last two nights.

I think maybe I'm just too nervous, or something. I mean, even as old as I am, I can almost get in a panic when I'm home alone. There are all these noises. Things thumping in the attic and all this shuffling and scraping in the basement. Sometimes it's all I can do to keep from running over to the neighbors. And I guess I probably would, but I wouldn't know what to say to them when I got there.

"Oh, I just thought I'd come over and see if your TV is still working or how your house plants or doing." I'd feel like a jerk.

Can You help me? I don't want to go through life in a panic. I don't want to spend the rest of my life running from noises and looking under the bed. Supppose I have to live alone when I'm older? What will I do? I'd have to hire a full-time, live-in security guard, or get a police dog, or something.

I'm not asking You to make me brave. I know that could never be. I'm just not cut out to be the first woman into combat or anything like that. But maybe You could help me be a little stronger, a little less pushed around by my fears, a little more dependent on You.

I'd like that.

I know You love me and will care for me, no matter what. But that doesn't always take care of my nervous imagination, which will probably still be wondering about a very skinny dead body under my bed tonight.

One good thing. So far, for all the looking, I've never found one there.

Thanks.

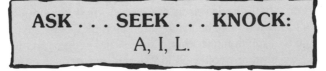

ASK . . . SEEK . . . KNOCK:
A, I, L.

10

BUT NOBODY'S PERFECT

Lord Jesus,

I wish I could get to sleep. Sometimes just lying here is so boring. The more I shut my eyes, the less sleepy I feel. And the more I think about getting up and reading or doing homework, the tireder I get.

Well, how did I do the past couple of days? Do I dare to think about that?

I was gonna get that history report done this weekend—at least get it started. I think it's due Thursday. That's four—well, really only three more days. Should be able to get it if I get to the library tomorrow. I should have started it, but there was all that other stuff to do and, after all, nobody's perfect.

Boy, Mom was on my case today. I don't know what was bugging her. Sometime she gets these really far out ideas. I mean, what was all that about getting out the old photographs? I guess I shouldn't have said that was a stupid idea. Maybe the idea wasn't too swift, but she looked kinda hurt when I said what I did. I don't mean to hurt her. I tried. I did pretty good the rest of the weekend and, after all, nobody's perfect.

Did Dad tell me to wash the car? I know he said something

35

about it during that gymnastics program this afternoon. I don't think he was really telling me to. He just said some stuff about how it would be nice if someone did it. I suppose he'll yell at me tomorrow when it's not washed. But what does he expect? I'm not the local slave around here. He could wash it too. I guess I would have washed it if I had remembered. Sometimes it's so hard to remember the stuff I'm supposed to do. But, after all, nobody's perfect.

Oh yeah, I was gonna call June, wasn't I? Poor June. Having all that trouble with Steve. She just can't seem to get him to get serious. She thinks I should know what to do about it. I can't even get anybody to date me, and I'm supposed to give her advice on how to get serious with Steve. She sure looked shocked when I told her off there after school. But sometimes she bugs me to death. I get so tired of hearing her complain all the time. It just gets too much. I meant to call her and apologize. She probably thinks I hate her now. And . . . Well, I wish I would have called, and it's too late now, isn't it? I usually remember, and, after all, nobody's perfect.

And I have got to stop yelling at my little brother. I mean, I must have looked like a complete jerk out there in the front yard screaming at him like that. But he makes me so mad. He does such unbelievable things. And of course, I always end up screaming, just like he wants me to. I did pretty good that other time though, when he changed the TV channel right in the middle of my program. I didn't scream or anything. Just calmly turned it back. I handled that okay, and, after all, nobody's perfect.

I guess when you add it up, I didn't do too well this weekend. I made Mom feel bad and yelled and my brother—when I going to. I left June hanging and forgot a job or two I was supposed to do. And I got most—well, some of my homework done.

I wish I could do better. Can You help me? It seems like everything I want to do, I forget or put off, and the things I shouldn't do, the ones I promise myself I won't do anymore—they are just the ones I do over and over again.

They say nobody's perfect, but I must be the world's best example of that. Does everyone else feel the same way? Is everyone bothered by all of this stuff, or is it just me? Maybe I'm too weak. Maybe if I could be stronger, could get hold of myself

I could get it right. Then I could get my assignments done and my jobs done, and stop letting myself and others and You down.

But I don't think I'm gonna be able to change very much. I've been trying for such a long time.

I'm sorry. I know I let You down. You and I both would like me to do better.

I know You will forgive me. And I know You will love me and trust me, even when I don't love and trust You very well.

Help me start tomorrow sure that as far as You and I are concerned the mistakes are all taken away. And help me do better.

I'd really like to.

I guess I'll never be perfect, but because You keep on loving me it helps to know its not too much to ask that You and I don't give up on me.

Thanks.

ASK . . . SEEK . . . KNOCK:
D, V, Y.

PIZZA

Lord Jesus,

Remember that TV program that showed some guy trying to get off heroin? He was all sweaty and shaky, and he looked very green. It was pretty hard to miss the point—heroin hooks you. And when you are hooked on heroin, you're really hooked.

There's not really much of a chance I'd try heroin. I mean, even if I could get it, I couldn't afford it. How much heroin can you get on five dollars a week for washing your dad's car?

Besides, You and I know I already have my little hook, and it really has me hung up.

For me it's not drugs or booze—it's pizza. When I go to a pizza place, I not only eat a couple of pizzas by myself, I also eat the pan, the tablecloth, the napkins—well, practically, anyway.

And not just pizza. Any food. If I could, I'd probably carry a little refrigerator around with me just to have something to gobble down every ninety seconds or so. And that's when I'm not even hungry.

It's not so much that I crave food—well, yes, I do crave it. But more, I just seem to need something in my mouth all the time. Anything will do. I mean, sometimes its really embarrassing. The other night we were at the pizza place—me and the guys. And there I was, picking up everyone's crumbs off of the table-cloth and eating them like some kind of an escapee from a concentration camp. I still can't believe I actually did that.

How can I get over this? It's like a huge war every day. Meanwhile I add pounds. Then I get uptight about eating too much—and when I'm uptight I eat even more, and add more pounds.

I have this horrible vision of myself in a few years getting weighed on a truck scale at a grain elevator. "Four hundred and forty-two pounds," goes the guy in the office there. "Pass the pizza," I go.

I really need Your help. I know You can't do a miracle and remove my appetite, but help me to do something positive about it.

I know what I have to do—get centered on something besides food—which, of course, is easier said than done.

But I'd like to. I really need to.

Help me to get a plan together that will at least move in that direction.

Up to now I have had all the willpower of a wilted vine, but maybe we can do better. I say we, because I know that I won't be able to do it by myself.

I guess I'd better start with the past. Forgive me for my overstuffed mouth and overweight body. Help me know that in a real way, because of Your love for me, I am new today. The mistakes of yesterday are gone.

And let's go at it.

Give me power—You promised it to me, not to avoid food, I know that won't work. Not even to be skinny—that I'm not cut out to be. Just give me power to get off the hook.

And then maybe next Friday at the pizza place, I can eat a couple of pieces of pizza, horse around a little with the guys, and leave the crumbs for the bus boy.

I'd like that.

Thanks.

ASK . . . SEEK . . . KNOCK:
E, S, W.

DESIGNER
JEANS

Lord Jesus,

It's not like I waste a lot of money on clothes. I mean, compared to some of the other girls, I run around in rags—really! But still, Mom keeps making fun of me because I want these certain designer jeans.

I don't know, they just fit better than those other dorky things, and they look good.

"I just don't know why you just can't get these jeans that are on sale over here," goes Mom. "They're ten dollars a pair cheaper and they look the same to me."

And when I try to explain, it's, "Do you mean you're gonna spend ten dollars for some fancy stitching on the back pockets? When I was your age, I was lucky to have skirts and tops that matched—let alone had fancy stitching on."

Spare me, Mom.

She just doesn't understand. It's not the stiching. It's that when you wear good jeans it shows you care enough about yourself to wear something that isn't dragged in off the street.

It's the same reason you fix your hair or wear makeup. It's not to be ignorant or show-offy. It's to say you think you're

41

important enough, special enough to be worth something.

And we know, don't we, how often I feel worth almost nothing? When Mom yells at me, or when I fail another test, or when I feel like people hate me. I feel so empty—so . . . I don't know, like I should be wearing a sack over my head or something.

But if I believed that—really felt that way all the time I really wouldn't care what I wore. Like some burnout, I'd probably wear skuzzy stuff and just let my hair fly.

I just wonder if Mom would like that.

Can You help me be patient with her? I know she thinks she's teaching me how to take care of my money. Help me show her that what I wear, what I buy, how I look is important—without having to yell at her or make a scene.

And help me to be proud of myself in the right way. I want people to know that I think You did a good job in making me. And that even though I know I have my faults, that I am happy with what You have given me, and I am not going to put it down or complain all the time.

But help me too, not to depend too much on clothes or worry too much about how I look. Sometimes I get in such a panic about my hair or my outfit. And it really seems important then. But I know that I will never really feel good about myself just because I have the right haircut or right stuff on. I know I have to feel okay about me inside. And there You can help me.

I need to remember that You love me no matter what jeans I wear or how I fix my hair.

Help me know that on the inside, where I sometimes feel like a failure, or feel empty, or feel like a burnout. Help me remember that I am really a designer person. I mean, that I am specially made, just right, not with fancy stitching, but with Your mark of love and forgiveness.

I'd like that.

Thanks.

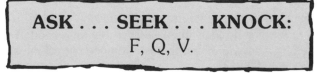

ASK . . . SEEK . . . KNOCK:
F, Q, V.

MY ROOM

Lord Jesus,

You know how my family, especially my mom, is really into this togetherness thing. Sometimes we almost drown in togetherness.

"Now we're all going to the photographer and get a family picture," goes Mom for the ninety-seventh time.

And we all get in the car together, and march into the studio together, and stand around and wait together, and smile for the camera together. And then Mom usually says that we ought to go shopping together or out to dinner together since we're "all dressed up anyway."

The whole thing is pretty weird. There I am with this whole gang of people moving like a parade around the store. And, of course, my mother keeps stopping here and there and asking me what I think of this dress or that pair of shoes. And meanwhile I'm trying to hide behind the clothes racks and pillars, hoping none of the kids from school see me.

I guess that's togetherness for Mom. I mean, all of us doing something at the same time seems to be some kind of a big deal for her. She talks a lot about those times, like she's afraid of when we won't be able to do them anymore.

And I can take it for an hour or two. But them I start to feel—I don't know. It's like feeling smothered or something. And it's all I can do to keep from yelling, "Why don't you all just leave me alone!"

"Why do you spend so much time in your room?" Mom asks when I come to the kitchen for a snack.

"I'm just studying," I say. But it's not really the truth. And she can't understand why I don't want to sit down with the rest of the family and watch some cutesy family program on TV. "Come on. It'll be fun," she goes.

And I suppose I hurt her when I go back to my room. But I just don't need all these people around me all the time. I have enough people pulling, pushing, and talking at me at school. I have enough of smiling and acting nice and being what other people want me to be.

In my room I can be myself and no one bugs me. When I need to be alone, my room is full enough with just me in it.

But, you know—it's kinda funny. For all the talk about togetherness around here, when I need somebody, I'm usually pretty much alone.

I mean, the folks are pretty good at talking about the weather and about this person and that—and real good at talking about what I should and should not be doing.

But when I'm hurt, when I feel like crying, when I get so mad I don't know what to do anymore, then they don't seem to have anything to say to me.

Then my room is so empty with just me in it.

And I wish my mom would come and sit on my bed and listen to me—maybe even hug me. I wish she'd care enough to leave the TV or whatever and just come and be with me.

But I guess I'm expecting a lot.

How is she supposed to know when I'm alone in my room and when I'm lonely in my room? How can she tell?

I wish so much she could. It's just not in me to say, "Mom come talk to me." I wouldn't know how to do that. And I don't know what she would say.

Can you help me? I guess I don't want you to make Mom any different. I mean, she is the way she is. And she loves me. I know that.

Make me more patient with her need to make memories. And help her be more patient with my need to be alone.

But most of all, help us to be better at letting the other know how we feel. Help us to reach out to each other. I think she'd like to too.

For all I know. Mom is out there wanting to come in and sit with me, even to hug me, and she doesn't know how to tell me.

Maybe You can help us learn to be closer to each other, not just when she needs togetherness, but when I need her to be with me.

Thanks.

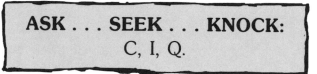

ASK . . . SEEK . . . KNOCK:
C, I, Q.

SHE
SAID NO

Lord Jesus,

How could it happen? She turned me down. She just stood there as with her chin poked out and said, "No, I'm sorry. I can't go with you Saturday. But thanks for asking."

How could she do that? Okay, so I'm no star in the looks department. But she's no knockout either. She's just some plain, dumb old girl.

Dan said she was a jerk. I should have listened.

I practiced that little asking speech a hundred times—two hundred, I don't know. Maybe that was it. Maybe it sounded too much like a line. I probably sounded like one of those talking soda machines. "Thank you for your money—please make your selection."

Well, she made her selection and her selection wasn't me.

What does she want? I mean I'm not some kinda greaseball or anything. Most of the kids at school like me. Some of them even think I'm pretty funny when I want to be. I can talk and all and I don't wipe my nose on my sleeve. What does she expect? The captain of the football team?

She's not that far from being a dog herself. I wouldn't even have asked her except she kept hanging around all the time. I thought she wanted me to. How was I supposed to know that she was just waiting there to flip her head around and buzz off down the hall leaving me standing there like some poor reject?

"Why don't you ask some other time," she goes as she bugs off.

I'll tell you this for sure. The end of the world will come before I ask her for the time of day again. If she thinks I am going to go through this again, she can just dream on.

And how do I face her? What do I say to her tomorrow? She and all her weird little friends are probably around her locker right now laughing at me.

How will I even go to school tomorrow?

And the guys. They all knew I was going to ask her. What do I say to them?

"Well, she said she was busy. Tough for her."

Doesn't sound very convincing.

How about, "Her grandmother died and she has to go to the funeral."

I guess that would be all right if they didn't find out that I haven't a clue as to whether she even has a grandmother.

I guess I'm really not so mad at her. I mean, maybe she did have somewhere else to go. But it would have been easier if she would have just explained it to me, or encouraged me a little. Would that have been too much to ask?

It's so hard for me to get up the nerve to ask a girl anyway. And then when I do, this kinda thing happens.

I don't know, maybe I just don't have it. I mean, maybe I'm one of those guys who just has to learn to go through life alone.

Spare me! It sounds like a soap opera.

Can You help me? I don't want to get down on her—and I especially don't want to get down on myself.

Help me know that I am not important or special because someone else thinks so or tells me so or even pays any attention to me.

I am worth something because You made me and You love me. I may not be what girls think is good looking or cute. But that doesn't mean I'm worthless.

Help me like myself, even be proud of myself in spite of **47** girls that don't have time for me and people that don't notice me.

It will not be easy this time. It would be easier to hide, to skip school, to stay to myself. But I know that won't help.

Make me strong enough to hold my head up, to smile, even to laugh. Don't let them know that she hurt me—because then the hurt would be double.

I know You love me and will not give up on me. Help me remember that's enough to make it possible for me to walk straight and tall and to have the nerve to ask some other girl some other time, even though she might say no to me too.

But maybe You could help one of them to say yes.

I'd like that.

Thanks.

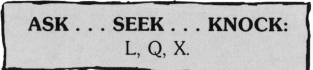

ASK . . . SEEK . . . KNOCK:
L, Q, X.

ABOUT ANGELS

Lord Jesus,

I want to go over this with You. Something kind of important happened. At least I think so, anyway.

At first, when it happened, I thought the motor fell out or something. There was this bang or thump and the car went all crazy.

I thought my heart would stop before the car did. Then I thought my heart wouldn't stop pounding.

It was just a flat tire. A very flat front tire.

I remember thinking, "How could this happen? I mean, at least four people drive this car all the time. How come they don't get the flat? Why does it have to be me? And why on this expressway with the cars flying by?"

Nobody stopped. I just stood there looking at this poor deformed tire.

I didn't know which way to walk to get help.

I tried to remember that time Dad said, "You have got to learn how to change a tire." And he dragged me out in the yard and showed me all this stuff about a jack and a wrench and what you put where.

49

All I could remember was that he sweated a lot.

I know all my I-am-capable-and-can-do-as-well-as-the-guys girlfriends would be very disappointed in me, but I couldn't make head or tail out of that junk in the trunk. There was this bar thing that I think Dad used on the screws or whatever on the tire, and this scissors looking contraption that I assume was the jack. But what came first?

I know I asked for a lot of help, I was thinking it would have probably helped more if I would have paid more attention when Dad had tried to explain it all to me.

Just as I was trying the jack for the fifth time, that huge shadow fell on me.

There was this guy, you know. From on the ground he looked like he was about eight feet tall. And he had greasy pants on and a beard. He looked like a Russian wrestler or an escaped convict.

I tried to scream, and I couldn't even get my legs to move to run away.

But his voice was soft. "Can I help, Miss?" he said.

What else could I do? I probably couldn't outrun him, even if there was somewhere to run to. And screaming would have gotten lost in the traffic noise.

I tried another prayer—remember?

"It seems to be flat," I said.

"Here, let me," he said.

It was like a miracle. I mean he knew just where to put that jack and how to work the bar and before I knew it, he had the spare on.

"Thanks," I go. It was kind of a weak little word. "Can I pay you something?" which was a dumb thing to say because I still don't know if I even had any money.

"Nah," he goes. "It's all right. But if I were you I'd get going. Kinda dangerous around here."

He was telling me!

I guess the whole thing could have been a lot worse. What if he had been somebody who would have . . . But I don't like to think about that.

And in a way it turned out for the best, you know. Today I took another tire-changing lesson. And I paid attention. I've got all the steps written down on a little card in the glove compartment. And I know what the wrench is for and where the jack goes.

I wonder how much You had to do with all of this. A lot, I suppose. I didn't think much about it at the time, but the right guy sure stopped when I needed him.

Not only did he want to help, he knew how, and he didn't even take any money for his trouble.

Almost like my guardian angel.

Thanks.

ASK . . . SEEK . . . KNOCK:
M, O, T.

BODY
BUILDING

Lord Jesus,

The other day that goon Harvey was showing off—You know how he does. He picked up this girl—and she's no flyweight, believe me. And he kind of waved her around in the air for a while. She got all red in the face and everyone ooohed and aaahed about how strong Harvey was.

If I tried to pick up even Angela, I'd probably dislocate my whole body—and You know how small Angela is.

I know we've been over this before, but while most guys are "big framed and muscular" as they say. I'm more . . .

Well, Mom, who always tries to be kind, says I'm "slight." What she means is that I'm little and skinny. I mean, you know what the comedians at school say:

"If you turn sideways your shadow disappears."

"If you'd put on a big hat, you'd look like a thumbtack."

"Wind's picking up, better nail your shoes to the floor."

And other real intelligent things like that.

Dad says, in his best advice-giving voice, he goes, "Build yourself up. You may be small-boned, but you could carry a lot more muscle. Just build yourself up."

The other day I looked in on one of those body building gyms. It was full of these big lumpy guys that have so much muscle you'd think their clothes would explode when they bend over.

The thing that bothers me is that when they are doing all this body building, they seem to be in such pain. Maybe they enjoy pain, I don't know. But, personally, I think anyone who's into pain is a little strange in the head.

Me. I hate it. See, that's just it about exercise. It's not the lifting and all that's so bad. It's the pain.

And Dad says, "Now everything worthwhile requires work and effort."

Yeah, Dad. Right you are. But is all this worthwhile?

I mean, I worked out for a couple of weeks, every other day, just like I was supposed to. I struggled through the pain and did all the huffing and puffing.

I didn't notice any difference at all. My shirts are still mostly full of air, and the only buldges I could find were on my shins, where I hit them with the weights.

I know I shouldn't complain. I mean, on the plus side, I am healthy and all of that. I have all the parts of my body in the right places and everything works. And some people say that my face is even a little good looking, in a small way, if you know what I mean.

But I sure would like to be bigger.

Can You help me?

I'm not asking You to make me magically into a muscle man. I know that would be silly.

But help me make up my mind.

Help me decide if I really do want to be bigger and stronger, and if I do, then give me the patience to work through the exercises and the pain to get there.

And if I decide I don't want to be more bulky, help me be more satisfied with the way I am.

Maybe some of us were just cut out to be small. Not everybody can be captain of the football team, or a weight lifter—or even be strong enough to lift a girl off her feet.

I need Your help to like myself better, to work on what I am good at and to be proud of what I can do, instead of ashamed of what I can't.

53

I guess no matter what I might be, I could always find someone who was stronger, better, faster, more, handsome—whatever.

What I need to learn, with Your help, is to be glad for what I am and to stop feeling bad when I come up short in comparison to someone else.

Good old Mom always says, "The really good things come in small packages."

I'd like to believe that.

Thanks.

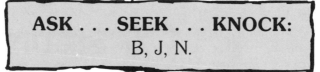

ASK . . . SEEK . . . KNOCK:
B, J, N.

SITTING
WITH MOLLY

Lord Jesus,

I wish I knew what to tell her, how to help her. Molly has so much hurt in her. What can I do for her?

We sit and she talks and cries. Sometimes I just give her a hug. I don't know what else to do.

Molly's a nice person. I like her. But she's so much like a hurt little bird. Everything destroys her. A bad grade, a look from someone she doesn't understand, something she can't do as well as others—sometimes just a word from a teacher and she's wiped out.

It's like she's all broken inside and just can't find any way to put the pieces back together again.

And the guys are no help. They tease her. They keep ragging her about her crying jags.

"Hey, Molly," they say. "What're we gonna cry about today?"

And, of course, Molly cries.

Molly tells me about the really grim stuff that happens at her house. I guess it's pretty bad. Her dad and mom don't get along at all, and there's a lot of yelling and hitting. Maybe that's why Molly hurts so much, I don't know. But she cries a lot about her home.

She talks about quitting school. I don't know what she'd do, or where she'd go. Last summer she ran away from home, but I think she was too scared to go very far. She wandered around all night and ended up at my house. She didn't call her folks for a while even after she got there. They didn't seem to care very much.

Molly dreams about some guy that is going to come and fall in love with her and take her to live in a nice little house with a grassy yard where she can play—almost like she was still a child. And he's gonna love her and make her safe. The trouble is, there aren't many guys like that around. But I don't want to remind Molly about that.

I hope she doesn't think the first guy who smiles at her is Prince Charming or something—and end up with more yelling and hurting.

Once Molly talked about killing herself. That really scared me. But she did it so matter-of-factly. Just said words about this way of killing herself and that, and which would be the best. I didn't know what to say. I tried to tell her she had a lot to live for. But she just cried. I ended up telling her that I loved her, and that seemed to help a little.

Funny. No—not funny. Strange—but there are a lot of girls—guys too, I guess, like Molly at school. You can see the hurt in their eyes. And no one seems to be able to help them.

Can You help me help Molly? I'd like to.

I talk to her sometimes about Your love for her and about what You did for her. But most of the time it doesn't get through the tears very well. Once we said a prayer together. I think that was when her grandma died. Well, she listened to me say a prayer.

"Thanks," she said. But I don't know how much Molly prays by herself. Sometimes it seems like she's awful mad at You—I guess about the hurt and all. I don't think that's gonna be easy for her to get over.

Anyway, I'd like to be better at helping Molly and the rest of the kids like her. I'd like to know what to say. Maybe You could show me, or tell me.

Or maybe there isn't so much to say. Most of the time when

I'm sitting with Molly, I do a lot of listening. And maybe that's what's important anyway.

What seems to help her most is when I just hold her and let her cry. Maybe nobody else does that, I don't know.

Could You help Molly too? I know she doesn't talk to You very much and she never goes to church—and I guess she's still pretty mad at You. But I know You love her. And I know she needs Your help. Don't give up on her. Stay with her.

And I'll keep sitting with her, just to let her know we're both still there and still care. Okay?

Thanks.

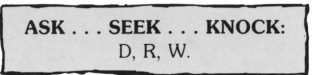

ASK . . . SEEK . . . KNOCK:
D, R, W.

SPEECH CLASS

Lord Jesus,

This guy must be crazy! He must think this is the only class I got this quarter. Doesn't he know I've got five other classes that are going to take a couple of minutes preparation some time or other?

What is he saying? Eight speeches, and a couple of them have to be six minutes or more. And read this book and that article and how many tests was that? Five—and a final. And memorize the phone book and write a five-hundred-page novel—well practically anyway.

Does he know how long it takes to get a speech together? I mean, I made a speech once—in grade school sometime. The teacher got some kind of a bug about getting us ready for high school, so we all had to make a five-minute speech. I think it took me two solid weeks to get ready for that. I must have practiced that thing about forty-five times—and when I got up in front of class, my mouth was paralyzed anyway.

Eight speeches! That will take me at least one year. And all I have is a quarter.

Why do they do this to us? I mean, *every teacher thinks*

their subject is the most important—and if we don't believe it they will pile on the work so that we are convinced.

Well, I'm convinced. Even if I start right now, there is no way I am going to get eight speeches written, memorized, and given this quarter.

Funny. That's what I thought last quarter about biology. I looked at the stuff we had to memorize. I mean there must have been four hundred terms to memorize and all of these little animals and cells and stuff that had these complicated names that all looked alike. I thought the chances of getting out of that class with anything over an F-minus was about one in a hundred. But I did it. I mean, we did it. I know You helped me. And Dad helped, and Kristi—she must have spent more evenings with me than she did with her boyfriend.

But I got a B, believe it or not. And I probably even remember some of those names, though I'm not sure how often arthropods or ornithoptera come up in everyday conversation.

But, I know I've gotta settle down here. Getting mad at the teacher over all the speeches and tests is not gonna get us anywhere.

The fact is, I did get through biology okay. And I did get through that speech back in seventh grade, or whenever it was. And so far I've been able to get all the weird assignments the teachers have asked for—well practically, anyway.

I need Your help though. I always want to worry about the whole thing, instead of taking it one part at a time.

Like Mom says, "No use trying to manage a month. Too much happens in a month. Just take care of one day at a time."

Sounds like a little sermon. And she says it mostly for herself, because if there is one thing she's not too good at it's taking things one day at a time.

But it's the right idea anyway.

We can get through this. I know I can write a speech, and I can probably give one if I don't get paralyzed mouth again.

And if I can do one speech, I can do eight. It just means I have to do them one at a time.

I'd like to ask You to write the speeches for me. That would be great—if I could open my notebook and see them all written there in a neat little pile with a paper clip on them. But I know that's not gonna happen. Probably wouldn't be good for me if it did.

But help me to do these crazy speeches the best I can one at a time.

And help me to keep my mouth working right when I have to give them.

Thanks.

ASK . . . SEEK . . . KNOCK:
K, I, Q.

THE FUNERAL

Lord Jesus,

Even though we weren't close friends, I thought Jim was a pretty good guy. I liked him. He wasn't what you'd call real popular, but everyone thought he was nice.

And he always got good grades, I guess. I mean he'd get A's and B's, at least on the papers I saw.

The guy that hit him didn't even know him. Just some drunken bum that couldn't keep his car on the right side of the road.

They said Jim didn't know what hit him. I guess that's supposed to mean he died right away. Some people seem to think that is a good thing to know.

Some of the guys and I sat near Jim's family at the funeral home for a while. We were his friends and felt like we wanted to be there.

Funny what people say at funerals. I guess they're trying to help, but if they'd think about it . . .

Maybe that's just it—they don't know what to say so they just say whatever comes into their head.

"At least he didn't suffer," a couple of people said.

What's that supposed to mean?

And this one old lady, in this real religious voice, said to Jim's mom, "Maybe the Lord wanted some young people in heaven and Jim was just the one He wanted."

What kind of a thing is that to say? I guess I don't believe that kind of stuff.

I mean, am I supposed to believe that You sent this bum into all those bars to get bombed and then aimed him at Jim so Jim would end up in heaven with You?

That means you send all the drunks into children and other innocent people; You make all the wars happen and send out the death squads, and cause all the other crazy things people do to each other.

Am I supposed to believe that?

If You are doing all the bad stuff in the world—what makes it bad, and what do we have to do with it?

I know some people believe that You push buttons or pull strings to make everything happen. I mean, even some of my friends. They think there's a big book somewhere and in that book you have a date written. Jim's date was two days ago. A big number came up and there goes old Jim.

Of course, I guess that is a very comfortable thing to believe. It kind of lets us off the hook. If we're just waiting around for our number to come up, then it doesn't really matter what we do, or how we live, or anything.

But that can't be right. If I get out and get drunk and run someone down—I did it, not You. Right?

And If I jump off a building—it's not my number that came up in the great death book in the sky. I'd die because I wanted to die. Isn't that right?

Or else why am I trying to do the right thing and taking care of myself? If You really do everything anyway, what did Jesus die for?

No. The drunk got himself drunk. He drove across the highway and he killed Jim. Whatever that nice old lady said, he is responsible—not You.

I'm not saying You don't protect us. I know You have helped me lots of times. There was that time on the ice, and that other time when I was small and I got in too deep at the pool.

62 But I guess Jim died because sin makes a lot of terrible things happen. Sometimes they happen to people we care about—sometimes to us.

I guess I'd like to say something to Jim's parents too. Something different from all that dumb stuff people say. Something like I say to myself, or I think You'd say to me.

I'd say, "I know God cares when you lose someone you love and you feel so terribly sad. I know He has Jim safe with Him, because Jim was one of His own. And I know He'll stay with us, even through this tough time."

I think something like that would be good for them to hear.

I'm not sure why that lady thought it would help them to think of You as a sniper, picking off kids like Jim before they had time to live.

But I think it might help them to know You love and care for them, and that You will keep them in spite of grief, or pain, or even death.

It helps me to know.

Help me let them know too.

Thanks.

ASK . . . SEEK . . . KNOCK:
E, H, J.

HE LOVES ME—
HE LOVES ME NOT

Lord Jesus,

I don't know what to do. Danny says if I really loved him I'd do it with him.

Not very original, I'm sure. Probably a million guys use that line every day. That's part of the trouble. Good old Danny doesn't even seem to want me enough to come up with a fresh line.

I don't know. I guess I ought to tell Danny to go take a flying leap somewhere. But when you get right down to it, I guess I care a lot about him.

We've been going together for so long, it seems like we've always been together.

He first asked me out when we were freshmen. And we were kinda awkward with each other at first. We only had about four dates in about six months. And I can't say I really liked him all that much. He was blushing all the time. And half the time he didn't seem to know what to do or what to say.

But now, I've gotten used to him. And he's real sweet in a way. He remembers things—anniversaries and stuff like that.

He brings me little gifts and he seems to be proud of me in front of his friends.

And it sure is great to have someone to do things with. I mean I would be bored to death if all I could do was sit around the house with my parents and watch TV—or something thrilling like that.

So I don't really want to drive him away.

I know too, this whole thing is no problem for a lot of kids. I mean a lotta girls are on the pill—their folks even get the stuff for them. And I guess they're surviving. They don't say much.

But I don't know. I just don't want it to be that way. Not that I think I'm so special. But I think that what happens between a boy and girl ought to be special.

My mom and dad gave me this big lecture about what could happen to me if I started sleeping around. And they were real stern about how I could get in trouble and how I'd have to answer to God for misusing my body and all of that.

I suppose the talking did them a lot of good.

But I guess it's not my folks or anything like that that makes me say no to Danny. It's more something about him.

When were alone and he holds me, you know, at first it's really nice, but then, when he gets excited, I get the definite feeling that I could be anybody—that it wouldn't matter to him what my name was, or who I was, or whether I even had a name.

Is that the way it's supposed to be? Is sex just some kind of exercise that you do with someone—and it really doesn't matter who it is?

I don't want it to be that way.

I remember that one time. It was at that party, wasn't it? And Bill was there. That was before he was even going with Janet. And all of a sudden, for no reason, he just leaned over and kissed me so nice and soft. It was like the brush of a feather. And he said, "You're a special person. Don't ever change."

See. That's what I think making love ought to be like. It ought to say that the other person is special. It ought to let them know in the best way possible that they are the greatest and most important.

But with Danny its all hard breathing and grabbing. I don't like to feel that I could just as well have a bag over my head

65

and be grabbed at. It makes me feel like a thing.

Well, I'm a person. And I want to be treated like a person—an important person. I am not a bean bag or a toy he can play with. And I don't believe that I have to let him treat me that way to show him I love him.

Can You help me?

I don't know how to handle this with Danny. I can't seem to make him understand. He thinks that I want to have the upper hand, that I want to be able to tell him what to do. How can I make him understand? How can I help him see that what we do when we're alone together is not about who can get his or her way. It should have to do with showing and telling love for each other.

Maybe I can't help him know that. Maybe he's seen so many movies or heard so many guys talk about "getting" girls and using them that there is no way for him to see it any other way.

It's such a shame. Our time alone together could be such a beautiful thing. If and when we were married. If we had that unused and untried way to show the most special kind of love for each other that any two people can have.

What is it going to mean if we marry—go through that whole grand ceremony and try to show each other a love that will last a lifetime by doing the same grabbing and hard breathing we've been doing in the back seat for years?

Well, he can call me what he wants and do what he wants. I need You to help me again. I want to try and help him understand again. But on this I won't change. I'm not going to become his grab bag just because he thinks he needs that or because he thinks he should be able to tell me what to do.

I don't care what he or the others say. I want the love and the sex that I have with that one guy I will marry to be more special than anything else I can do or have ever done.

I'm not going to settle for less for Danny or anybody else.

Help me stay with that promise to myself and to You without getting proud or vain about it. Help me be the kind of person You and I want me to be without acting like I was some kind of a fanatic about this whole thing.

But help me remember that I am a person, a worthwhile person. That I, like the people you give me to date, to love and maybe even to marry, deserve to be treated like we're something more that a convenient thing to make one another feel better once in a while.

And help me to find that guy who feels the same way.
I'd like that.
Thanks.

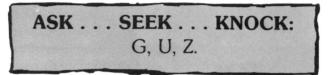

ASK . . . SEEK . . . KNOCK:
G, U, Z.

SHE LOVES ME—
SHE LOVES ME NOT

Lord Jesus,

Don't get me wrong. I think Betsy is a great girl. I mean, we've been going together for ages, it seems like. And we have a good time together, most of the time. She laughs a lot, and she always gets so embarrassed when I give her any kind of a gift.

In a lotta ways she's just the kind of girl I'd look for if I was going to try to find someone else. She likes a lot of the same stuff I do, and we think alike about most things.

But she's so—I don't know—cold, I guess. It's not that I expect a girl to hop into bed with me after the first date. I wouldn't even want her to do that. But sometimes you'd think I was personally insulting her if I even want to touch her.

Wouldn't you think we'd get past the kiss on the cheek stage after a year or two?

"There are things in life besides making out," she goes in her very pious voice.

Right you are, girl, but it just isn't natural not to get a little friendly after we have been out so many times.

68   I really care about her. And I like to be with her. But even more, I like to hold her—to touch her. What's so terrible about that? But the best she can do is kinda to put up with that for a while. Then all of a sudden she goes, "Stop grabbing at me. I'm not something you can grab. I'm a person."

Big news. I know she's a person. What's that supposed to mean? She acts like there is something wrong with me, like I'm some kind of animal just because I want to touch her.

Is that the way it would always be with her? I know that sex is not the most important thing in life. But it is important. And if you love someone you ought to like to be with them, to touch them with more than a handshake. Or else what is married life all about?

I don't want to spend my life with someone thinks she can jerk me around by the nose because she decides when and where and even if we can make love. I don't want to spend the rest of my life on trial, to see if I'm good enough to sleep with.

What kind of a life would that be?

She says she cares about me, but I really don't know. If she cared, would she keep backing away from me all the time? Would she look at me as if I was some kind of scum just because I wanted to hold her or to touch her? What kind of love is that?

I don't know what to do. I hate to force myself on her. But how can I find out if she cares about me or if she is just using me to keep from getting bored until someone else comes along who she really might like—and then she'd drop me like I had the plague.

Can You help me? Can You help me understand her? What is going on with her? Does she think she's too good for me? Does she think she's so special that I will never be able to touch her, even if we were married? Does she really love herself so much that I won't even have a chance?

Can You help me let her know I care without sounding like I'm begging her to care about me?

I know I'm not very smart about these things. And my dad tells me that if a girl tries to get the upper hand before you're married you're going to have a terrible life after. But I don't think it should have to be that way. Why should one or the other of us have the upper hand? Can't we just love each other and show that love to each other? Do we have to make a contest out of **69** it and see who says yes and who says no and when it's all right to say yes and when not?

It seems to me that making love ought to be more special than that.

I need Your help to know what to do about this. Maybe I should look around for someone else who would be more like me—or more like the kind of person I'm looking for. Someone who was more able to show her feelings and less tied up about sex.

But I don't want to let her go. I care too much.

I wish You could solve this one for me. It would be great if You could just give me a sign, or give me the answer.

I guess I'll have to keep trying to get through to her, and try to understand her.

Give me the wisdom and strength to know what is right and to see what is right in her.

Help me show her that I really care about her. I think that would help her. And maybe if I could show her, she might be able to accept me and even my touches as ways to say my love for her.

I'd like that.

Thanks.

ASK . . . SEEK . . . KNOCK:
G, U, Z.

MOM

Lord Jesus,

You know how really good Mom is. Oh, I know she's not about to sprout wings or a halo or anything like that. I know she has her faults, for sure. Sometimes she gets all rattled and ends up yelling about stuff that isn't very important. And sometimes she's on my case for days when she can't seem to get to the point of what's bugging her. And she forgets things.

But all in all, she's a really good person. She cares about other people and cares about me. She tries to do the right thing all the time—to help instead of hurt and to be kind instead of just talking about it like a lot of people do.

And she makes me so ashamed.

She must be the most religious person in the world. She seems so sure You are there. For her, it's like You're another person who lives in the house, who's a part of the family.

And she's always saying things like, "God willing," and "We have so much to thank God for," and "We just have to take more time for our devotions," and all like that.

I really wouldn't be surprised if she set out an extra plate for You at the table and spent a half an hour praying before every meal.

Funny. I find myself getting mad at her when she says and does all those things. Not that I'd want her to be any different. I'm glad for her. Knowing You as well as she does seems to make things easier for her—like she is more confident, less afraid of what might happen.

What bugs me, makes me feel ashamed, is that I'm not that way at all. For all her trying to teach me about You and trying to show me how to pray and think of You all day, it doesn't seem like her way of doing things has rubbed off on me, at least not very much.

Oh, You know how it is. I try to say my prayers at night and I even read my Bible sometimes, and I thumb around in some of those strange little prayer books people have given me.

But half the time I find myself wondering if You are even really there at all, or if You are there, if You hear me.

I seem to feel so far away from You so much of the time.

For some reason, even though people always say we are "so much alike," Mom's up-front religion doesn't fit me very well. I try to think of You as there beside me, but it just doesn't seem real for me.

And I try to use words like "God willing" and "I'm so thankful to God," but they don't sound right when I say them. They sound so phony, even to me—I bet they sound downright jerky to other people.

What can I do? I've tried to be better at all this religion stuff. I've tried to imagine You closer, to say longer prayers, to think of You more often, but it just doesn't seem to work for me.

Can you help me? I don't know what else to do.

I ought to talk to Mom about it. But I don't think she'd understand. What would she say if I told her that half the time I'm not even sure You are there, let alone that You care? She'd probably have a heart attack right on the spot.

I wonder if she ever felt this way? Did she ever wonder or question or look for You when she couldn't find You? Did she ever feel like she was praying to the empty sky? I wish I knew.

I need You to help me.

Don't get me wrong. I'm not asking for a miracle that would all of a sudden turn me into some kind of a religious fanatic or anything like that. I don't even know if I want to be as showy about my faith as Mom. But I would like to be surer of Your being with me. I'd like to have more confidence that You are there and that You hear me when I pray. I'd like to be able to depend more on You during the day. I sure have trouble depending on other people, or even on myself.

I know it won't happen like a flash of light or anything dramatic like that. But don't give up on me either.

Maybe You could help me see You in some of the people who keep on loving me and keep on forgiving me. Maybe You could touch me once in a while through them, to kind of wake me up to what You are doing to me and through me.

I know that You said that You would be with me. Help me know that better—a little bit more like my mom knows it.

I'd like that.

Thanks.

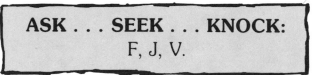

ASK . . . SEEK . . . KNOCK:
F, J, V.

MY PLAN

Lord Jesus,

Believe it or not, this guy Kyle gets up in history class the other day and he just lays out a plan for his whole life right there in front of everybody.

It was amazing. I've never heard anything like it. And I don't even know who asked him to do it or why he thought he should. But all of a sudden, there he was saying he he was going to this or that college and study these subjects. He even knew how much all of this was going to cost him. The he told about the kind of a job he was going to get and what kind of house he was going to build. I bet he could have even told us the color of the rooms and what kind of doorknobs the place was gonna have.

I still can't believe he actually did that.

At first I thought he was completely weird or that his brain has spazed out or something. But the more I think about it, the more I wish I had a plan like Kyle's.

It must be great not to have to wonder about next year and the year after that and college and what is going to happen.

I mean, wouldn't it be fine not to have to stand there

tongue-tied like some kind of a jerk when people ask you what you are going to do "when you grow up."

I haven't a clue. Not even a guess.

I know there are a couple things I'd like to do. I'd like to be a cross-country truck driver. I think it'd be great to see everything and stop at truck stops and just bang around. But how do you tell that to the guidance counselor who wants to know your "future plans"?

And I think it might be OK to own a business—to be your own boss. I mean, after you got the hang of it and some good help, you'd have lots of free time to do what you want. And if the business made money . . .

My problem is, I just don't know what kind of business I'd like to spend the rest of my life at. I mean, what if I got into something like hardware? Could I stand to spend year after year explaining to Grandma Somebody why she should buy this faucet or that one?

Spare me!

So I'm probably going to keep falling into my future year by year—kind of playing it by ear.

I suppose I'll go to college and study something.

I try to think about what it would be like to study one thing for four years in college. What if it was English? Who would want to know that much about English? And if you did, what would you do with a head full of that kinda stuff?

And then I think about "doing something for mankind." as some people say. Maybe I could be a social worker, or a therapist, or maybe a teacher—though I'm not sure I could stand being around kids all the time. I mean, they're so dirty and noisy and their noses are always running.

But, anyway, serving mankind, or whatever, sounds very good, but I don't think it pays very well. And how many years yet in school?

Can You help me?

I mean, I don't think I need a plan down to the last doorknob about what is going to happen in the future. But I think I could use a general direction, anyway.

Maybe You are waiting for me to make up my own mind. Remember that kid who used to deliver frozen food to our house? He was getting ready to go to college for about ten years, waiting for You to tell him which college to go to. I suppose you can wait your whole life away like that.

I suppose I'm not so worried about which college I go to or even if I go at all. And I'm not worried about what I do when I'm "grown up." But I would like to find somewhere where I would fit in and find something to do that wouldn't be completely a waste of time and boring on top of it.

Can You help me find that place and that thing to do? Some place, some job that will make me feel like my life is worthwhile? I mean, I don't have to get any awards for self-sacrifice.   And I sure don't need to be rich and famous. But I would like to feel like it made some difference that I lived and worked and found my place. I would like to know that what I did while I lived mattered—that I made something happen that was important to at least a few people. That someone would remember that I had been there, and be glad for what I had done.

Can You help me find that place?

I'd like that.

Thanks.

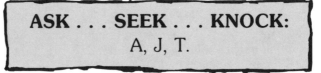

ASK . . . SEEK . . . KNOCK:
A, J, T.

DON'T DO WHAT I DO . . .

Lord Jesus,

I know I complain a lot, but this really bugs me.

In the past couple of days my parents have given me lectures on how bad beer parties are, how dangerous smoking is, how important it is for me to tell the truth, and how terrible it is when I raise my voice when I am talking to them. They tell me that it is disrespectful for me to yell at them, and that if I have something to say, I should say it quietly and "with a respectful tone."

Meanwhile, my dad just finished a beer and a cigar, while he was on the phone telling some guy that he couldn't meet him for lunch tomorrow because the family is going on a picnic together. We haven't gone on a family picnic for five years. And all of that followed a hollering match during which he did all the yelling at me for not cleaning up my room again.

Now I suppose that adults have certain rights just because they are adults. I suppose that since they own the house and pay the bills, they are entitled to do things the way they want to.

But it seems to me that things ought to at least be fair. If **77**

I'm not supposed to drink and smoke—should they? And if I'm not supposed to lie—is it all right for them to do it? And if I'm supposed to speak respectful to them—shouldn't they do the same for me?

Are children just around to act like adults think they ought to act?

I know I'm complaining, but it just doesn't seem fair.

And the worst part about it is, I don't know that I can do much about it.

I tried to talk to my dad a couple of times, but he gets pretty excited if he thinks I'm accusing him of being unfair, or if he thinks I'm trying to tell him what to do.

He never says it, but the program is pretty much "Don't do what I do, do what I say."

I'm not asking You to change my parents—to suddenly turn them into saints, but I guess I'm asking You to help me get them to understand.

I don't know how we are going to do it. I've already tried the direct approach. And the other way might cause a whole lot of trouble.

I mean, I just don't know if Dad will get it if I yell at him and then say something like, "Well, you yell at me." That might get me a smack in the mouth.

And if I go to Mom, she probably won't even catch onto what I'm talking about. She thinks I complain too much already.

I have to leave this to You.

First, help me stop worrying about this thing. I'm only going to cause myself more grief. Let me pay attention to how I am living and acting, and less attention to what they are doing.

Help me understand them. I guess they have their problems too. And I guess all the rules they lay down for me, even the ones they don't keep themselves, are for my good—as they say.

Help me forgive them when they hurt me. And forgive me when I resent them, get angry, and hold a grudge against them.

Most of all, help me be smart enough to get through to them—not just so the rules will be more fair, but so that they will have a chance to be the kind of Christians they want me to be, and the kind You want them to be too.

78   Thanks.

ASK . . . SEEK . . . KNOCK:
C, P, S.

FORGIVING FRAN

Lord Jesus,

I knew it would happen again. The trouble is, I never seem to learn. Fran is such a likable person. I really enjoy being around her, doing things with her. And she seems to need the attention I give her.

But it happens every time. Just about the time I think we are getting close—really getting so we can trust each other, she seems to set out to hurt me. All of a sudden I hear these terrible things she's saying about me. Or she'll tell something I told her to keep a secret. It's almost like she does it just to see what I will do.

But I can't figure out why. Why does she do it? Does she really hate me? But if she does, why does she bother with me at all? Why does she spend all that time with me if she is really mad at me, or if she really doesn't like me?

I guess I can't understand it at all.

Maybe she is testing me—seeing if I will stick with her, even when she does these ignorant things.

I asked her about it. I mean, I went straight to her and told her what other people said she was saying. But she denied it.

She said she had never said anything of the sort. I don't know. I guess she is lying. But why?

She tells me everything, I don't think she makes it up, about all the terrible stuff that has happened to her since she was small. Her real father really treated her bad. And when he left, the bunch of guys that used to be her "uncles" for whatever weeks or months her mom needed them, didn't treat her much better. I know some of them did bad things to her. She never says just what, but you can see the hurt in her eyes when she talks about it.

I guess all of that has something to do with what she does to me. But I wish I could understand better.

What should I do now? Should I forgive her again? She didn't really admit she had done wrong. But she did ask me to be her "best" friend again.

Maybe she is so sure that she is unlovable, she doesn't trust even people who say they like her. It's almost like she has to test me and her other friends to see if we will really stick by her— even when she does these completely weird things.

Well, I don't know if it is worth it anymore.

I think maybe I should just give up on her. I've been hurt enough. I've had her turn on me too many times. I've had it. She can just find someone else to stick the knife in.

But I don't want to give up on her.

Can You help me forgive her again? I know I can't do it without Your help.

Peter once asked You how many times he should forgive someone. And You said seventy times seven. But that's pretty tough.

I need Your help. I don't want to give up on Fran. I know she's a good person—one of Your own. But it is so hard to stick with it when she acts the way she does.

Help me forgive her one more time. I know it will not be harder than Your forgiveness for me again and again and again.

And give me understanding. Help me know what is happening with Fran. So I can help her, and love her, and forgive her. Even if she can't forgive herself.

And help me know how to say to her that she is special, loved by You and all of us, even if she doesn't feel that way inside.

81

Then maybe she will be able to trust the friendship and the love we have for her.

I'd like that.

Thanks.

ASK . . . SEEK . . . KNOCK:
B, R, Y.

DAD CRIED

Lord Jesus,

Dad was crying when I came home last night.

Even though I don't think I ever heard him do that before—not even when Grandma died, I know he was in the living room crying by himself.

I didn't know what to do. What do you say to your dad when he cries? How can you help?

I know what's wrong. He's been laid off for so long now. And there just are no jobs. I guess he must've tried a hundred places.

He never talks to me about it, but I heard him telling Mom that they all tell him he's "overqualified" for almost every job he tries for. He thinks that the real reason they won't hire him is because of his age. And he's probably right.

It must be really bad for him to hear people tell him no over and over again. He must feel like he's not worth much any more. Maybe that was why he was crying, I don't know.

I know I startled him when I came in. He wiped his eyes real quick.

He told me it was "nothing." But I already knew it was something.

"Do you want to talk, Dad?" I said.

"No. It'll be all right," he goes.

I wonder why? Why can't he talk to me? I'd like to be able to help him. Not that I have any great ideas about how he could get a job. And I'm not sure that I could even do much for his sadness. But I'd like to try.

It's hard being left out. I hear the folks talking—arguing sometimes about this. I know Dad is feeling worse and worse.

He doesn't talk much at the table anymore. And he sits by himself a lot.

And he used to laugh.

Remember that time he played that silly joke on Mom— brought home that terrible looking hat he told her he had bought for her? And Mom doesn't even wear hats much.

And he played it real straight while she hemmed and hawed around trying to tell him that the thing looked like it was made by the mad hatter himself.

And they both laughed so hard when she put it on.

But he doesn't laugh any more. And I wonder if he thinks I don't notice.

Can You help me?

I'd like to be able to help my dad. He's always been so special. And I'd like to have him trust me enough to let me listen to him, even cry with him.

I feel so shut out when he doesn't talk to me.

I suppose he thinks I'll think he's weak if I see him cry or hear him complain. Maybe he thinks he has to pretend that he's real strong so I'm not afraid.

But I'm more afraid of being left out of his problems and closed out of his life. I know he feels alone. Just like I felt so alone when he cried and couldn't talk to me.

Maybe You could help me reach out to him in a way that he could accept. Maybe you could help me say the right words or ask the right questions, or just be there at the right time.

Maybe You could help me let him know that I won't think less of him because he hurts and shows it and because he cries. Help me know how to show him that what we share now might be more important than all the talking we have done before.

I'm not asking for some great miracle. Just help us reach each other better.

I'd like that.

Thanks.

ASK . . . SEEK . . . KNOCK:
H, O, W.

27

MY MUSIC

Lord Jesus,

This whole thing started when I bought my stereo. I mean, before I didn't have a chance, with Dad always playing that weird music on the stereo in the living room.

Now I've tried to understand that stuff he plays all the time. I mean, some of it sounds pretty okay—kinda sweet and sappy. But my problem is that it all sounds the same. It seems like all you hear is violins going up and down and up and down, and every once in a while somebody bangs around on a drum.

And there's no beat—no rhythm to it. It's just all these instruments going up and down and around together over and over again. I just can't figure it out.

And the really weird thing is that when I play my music on my stereo, Dad goes, "Turn that racket down!"

What makes my music racket and his music music? It sounds like racket to me.

I asked him about it. He goes, "All that stuff you play sounds the same. All you hear is guitar chords and drums. Lots of bass and lots of beat and no one can understand the words."

I can.

I gotta admit that some of the words aren't too brilliant, and they do repeat a lot sometimes. But at least the music goes somewhere. It just doesn't wander around there in the air. It says something, even if it isn't much.

For a while my Uncle Al was real big on the rock-music-is-a-tool-of-the-devil kick. He about had my mom convinced. He brought over these tapes that were supposed to show how some kind of evil message was being sent backward when a couple of rock songs were played.

It's not all that easy to understand what these guys are trying to sing when you hear it frontwards—so I'm not too sure what a message that is recorded backward is supposed to do. But Mom got all excited about it for a while. Then we really had a hassle.

She spent a couple of hours listening to my records, trying to figure out what evil stuff they were singing about. I don't think she understood any of the words, and the music gave her a headache, so she gave up on that.

Sometimes my dad and I end up yelling at each other about the music we listen to. And when you think about it, that's pretty stupid.

I mean, why should we run each other down because we like different things?

Forgive me when I am hardheaded and insist on my own way.

Help me be more patient with his kind of music. Maybe You could help me see a little bit of what he sees in it. It must be pretty important for him, or he wouldn't play it all the time.

And help him be a little more patient with what I like—not only in music, but in clothes, hair styles, and all the other stuff we disagree on.

Can You help us both listen to each other a little better and not be so quick to make fun or to run down the other person?

It is so easy to think I'm right and that he is some old-timer who is completely out of it.

And I guess it is real easy for him to see me as some kind of a young "smarty pants" as he calls it, trying to tear down everything that he thinks is important.

I know we won't be able to make each other change—but maybe we can be better at understanding one another and listening to one another and appreciating the other—even if we don't agree.

I'd like that.

Oh, and by the way, maybe we'd better start that listening stuff with me.

Thanks.

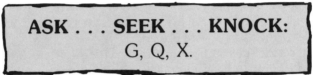

ASK . . . SEEK . . . KNOCK:
G, Q, X.

LITTLE BROTHERS
AND OTHER PESTS

Lord Jesus,

I'd like to talk to You about this "loving others" business.

I mean, that's not so tough if You are talking about loving the starving Africans or the people who have never heard of You in New Guinea or somewhere. I got all kinds of feelings of concern for people like that. And I'm the world's greatest sucker for any sob story. If they talk about children in need in Borneo I'm ready to ship off my whole allowance in the next mail pickup. And any time they are gathering canned goods for whoever is hungry, I pack up every can we aren't likely to use in the next twenty minutes and haul it off.

See, I don't think it's hard at all to love those people out there. It's the ones around me I have trouble with.

Now don't get me wrong. Most kids are all right. I care about the gang I hang out with and I even like some of the guys at school who aren't complete jerks. Even most adults are okay if you don't have to spend too much time with them.

But there are some people who just drive me completely nuts. How an I supposed to love these weirdos?

First there's dorky old Nancy. I mean she's always hanging on me like a leech. And all she wants is to "take a little look at my notes to see if she missed anything in class." Missed anything! She hasn't taken a note in years. All she wants to do is to copy mine.

And speaking of copying. There's shifty-eyed Bruce, who doesn't even know how to do his own test papers. I mean, he must have stretched his neck about four inches just since he started high school. And he gets pretty good grades, wrecks the curve in most of my classes, and doesn't care about anybody but himself.

And Sal. She tries so hard to be my "best friend." But I can't stand her. She is always sending me these very sappy little notes about how important I am in her life and how much she needs me to be her friend. And she falls into little pieces whenever I even stop to talk to one of the other kids. Who needs that? I've got enough trouble.

And even worse is that guy Harold, believe it or not, who thinks he's some kind of a gift to all women of the world. I wonder if he broke his only mirror or if he is totally blind. And he does such unbelievable things—like pulling my hair or hitting my books out of my hands. And I am supposed to fall at his feet or something because he acts like a kindergarten dropout.

And worst of all is my little brother. The kid drives me crazy. He's in my room, in my things, following me around, taking my stuff, bothering me when I'm on the phone, hitting me, making faces at me, screaming at me, and whatever else comes into his flakey little head.

Now I know I'm supposed to love all these people. But it sure is hard.

How can I do it? I'd like to put them all in a large crate and ship them to Siberia. Then maybe, I'd be able to love them and send them a Care Package or something.

Can You help me? I really don't want to hate anyone. I know that You love me—and them too. And You want me to forgive even the people who do the same dumb stuff over and over.

But it's so hard.

Help me see past the stupid things they do to the person inside who is probably hurting and asking for help. Help me keep my temper and forgive me when I lose it and want to hit back.

And especially help me deal with my little brother. He'd try the patience of a saint—and we both know I have a long way to go before they call me that.

Keep on loving me and forgiving me, and I'll try to keep depending on You to help me love and forgive these too-close ones who put my patience, my love, and my good intentions to the hardest test.

Thanks.

ASK . . . SEEK . . . KNOCK:
C, D, N.

29

EIGHTEEN

Lord Jesus,

I can't figure out how I got to be eighteen already. I wonder what part of me is? My head sure isn't.

Most of the time I feel more like fourteen—or even less. I don't think I'm ready for eighteen yet.

Eighteen sounds so grown up—like you're supposed to be able to manage everything, and have everything together, and make all your own decisions and . . .

Some days I have a lot of trouble figuring out what I'm going to do with the next ten minutes—let alone the coming days or weeks.

And some days I can't even decide which top to wear, let alone making any great decisions about my future.

And my parents sure aren't ready for me to be eighteen. I don't know if Mom will ever get to the place where she can treat me like I was something other than twelve. She is still into the telling and the scolding.

"You can't even keep your room picked up, how can we send you off to college?" she goes.

I know she didn't expect an answer to that question, but

the tough part is, I wouldn't know how to answer it anyway.

I don't know how I'll be able to go off to college. I have no idea if I'll be able to do it. I may make a total disaster of it in the first quarter I'm there. And it won't be my messy room that does me in. It will be unmade plans, unfinished work, failed tests, and incomplete assignments.

I am so scared. My fourteen-year-old insides just don't know if they can handle all of this—being treated like eighteen and expected to act like that.

Mom keeps talking about "when you leave home," as if I was going to disappear out into the world or something. I can hardly stand it when she says that. I want to shout at her, "Mom, I'm still a little girl—your little girl. You can't send me away. I need to be safe in my room, to have somebody make my meals and hold me when I'm afraid and help me with my homework. I can't do it out there alone. I'm so afraid to be alone."

But then there are other times when the my parents do treat me like I was twelve. They scold and push me around and act like I was a helpless child. Then I can't wait to get away.

Can You help me? I need Your help with this.

Can You help me have more confidence in myself. I've always been able to do what's expected of me—even if it always isn't just on time. And I've always been able to make the decisions and to manage things pretty well—even if my folks aren't always too impressed. But it's not so important any more that they be impressed. I have to be convinced that I can do it. That I can make it. That I can manage.

Help me be more sure of myself, less tempted to run back into my room and hide. Give me the confidence I need to pack my suitcases and to "leave home," and make things work out there.

And help me know that that fourteen-year-old inside me is really able to function like an eighteen-year-old—even if she doesn't feel like one.

And let the part of me that will never leave home be a strong anchor to help me, instead of just a set of longing memories that make me feel homesick.

Together we'll get through the first day, the first week, the first test, the first term paper, the first quarter. And maybe I'll even surprise myself at how well I do.

93

But in any case, stay with me. I don't think I can manage this on my own.

Help me do well, but most of all, help me learn to feel comfortable about being eighteen. I guess I can handle being scared—but help me be able to laugh too.

I'd like that.

Thanks.

> ## ASK . . . SEEK . . . KNOCK:
> L, V, T.

30

TELEVISION

Lord Jesus,

I'm so mad at myself. I just spent the whole evening in front of that dumb box again. And the worst part about it, there was nothing worth watching.

Believe it or not, I watched three half-hour programs they call comedies. I don't think any of them even made me smile. I mean, there were a lot of people yelling at each other, and some others acting like complete jerks. It was about as funny as watching a tin can rust.

And then there was this "action" show, with some good-looking "detectives." There was a lot of action all right—a lot of chasing around and banging cars together. The only problem was, the commercials were more exciting and interesting than the program.

I don't know why I do that. I mean, why do I spend hours sitting there watching stuff that wouldn't entertain a mentally defective cocker spaniel? There are hundreds of other things I could be doing.

There's that good book that Meg gave me. I started it and never finished. And I should write to all those people who wrote

95

to me. And there's the history report that's coming due. I could always get started on it. And my room needs to be cleaned, and I should call all the kids on the committee to get that car wash for next weekend organized. And . . .

Instead I sit there with my baby-blues glued to the trusty old tube.

I guess it's just my most convenient excuse for not getting at what I have to do. I mean, all those other things take a little work, and sometimes I just can't seem to find the energy to make the effort. It's easier to let it all slide and tell myself I'll do it later— just so later never really comes.

And I guess I could make You and myself some wonderful promises about how I'm going to finally get myself organized and stop wasting time in front of the TV and do all those things I intended to do.

And I probably would even mean it.

But the trouble is, every one of those fine promises I make, even the ones I make on New Year's Eve, somehow last about as long as the dust stays off my dresser top.

I can promise and promise. And there I am again sitting glassy-eyed in front of the next exciting look into the life of some smart-mouthed kid who is boring everyone to death as he tries to figure out new ways to insult the adults trapped in the program with him.

Can You help me?

Not that I expect You to suddenly change me into this incredibly efficient doer of good deeds who is not only able to schedule time perfectly but also is able to get every job and assignment done a week before it is due. I guess that wouldn't be me.

But I would like to move toward a better use of my time.

First, forgive me for the hours and hours I wasted last night, and the night before that, and the night before that, and . .

Help me learn to go to bed at least a couple times a week with the feeling that the whole evening was something more than a TV wasteland.

And I will make this promise. The next time I find myself sitting in front of the TV, asking myself what in the world I am doing there, I will do everything I can to get up, shut the stupid set off, and look for something else to do—even if it isn't very creative.

And maybe You could help me both ask the question and, at least some of the time, get the set turned off.

I have to learn to do it some day. It might as well be now.

Wouldn't it be terrible to suddenly find myself old, with a television for my only friend, and the accomplishment of my life a million hours of nonstop viewing?

Spare me!

Please?

Thanks.

ASK . . . SEEK . . . KNOCK:
E, I, Y.

COLOR BLIND

Lord Jesus,

At my school we don't see that many people who are different—I mean different races and stuff like that. So when Mike showed up with that black guy at the track meet Saturday, I didn't know what to make of it—or of him.

I don't know what I expected. Maybe I thought he'd talk or walk different, or that he would automatically hate me because I was white. Maybe I thought he'd pull a knife and start to wave it around. I don't know.

But what bothered me was that the first thing I saw was that he was black.

Why is that? I didn't see a person who happened to be black. I saw a black person and didn't know how to take him.

I wonder how many years I'd have to be around blacks to see them first as people? How long would it take to get over the stupid attitudes I've been around all my life?

Oh, I don't mean my folks are out and out against black people—not like some. Some of the kids at school say completely dopey things about all blacks being dumb, and all Polish people being stupid, and all . . . But You know what I mean. And then there are those "jokes"—but we won't even talk about them.

Nothing like that happened while I was growing up—even among my relatives. It was just like we pretended that black people weren't really there. We never were around any. My parents don't even know any, I don't think. And when we saw them, it was always something like "Isn't it terrible how some people have to live," or "You'd think people would have more pride in their homes," or something like that.

But the message got through loud and clear: "These people are different." And it is so hard for me to get over that now. Lance turned out to be a pretty good guy. Fast! I mean, he could run! And I found myself thinking, "Maybe all of them can run better than we can." Which is another dumb thing to think. Probably some of them can run pretty fast—but some of them can't, I'm sure.

Lance talked a little about his family. It sounded just like mine. He was complaining that his mother wanted him home before dark and that she had fourteen jobs he was supposed to do before tomorrow. Sure sounded familiar. And I was surprised. I don't know what I expected.

Can You help me?

I need a lot of help with this. I know that if people keep seeing each other's skin color first and with all the suspicion and fear that goes with that—it will be a very dangerous world to live in. But even while I know that, I can't even get over the way I look at black people—the way I expect them to be and act different from me and my friends.

I guess I'm not asking for a miracle that will make me suddenly color-blind. I'm not sure that would even make sense. But I do need Your help to see people and not colors—to see each person as a person with talents and abilities, with faults and failings—to see each person as a self that You love, whatever his color or the way he wears his hair or the kind of clothes he wears or the way words come off his tongue.

And maybe You could help me get that good word out to other people who keep on saying dumb things about these people all being this way or that people all being something else.

There are probably a lot of important things I can do in my life. I guess letting people know about You is one of them. But it sure must be important to help myself and others know that **99**

You love each person without even looking at the outside. And that we who belong to You will want to do the same.

If all of us could get that simple word out, the whole world might be better, fairer, and safer.

Meanwhile, help me to care about Lance because he's a good guy, a good runner, and a good friend.

Thanks.

ASK . . . SEEK . . . KNOCK
F, S, M.

HE SAID
THAT SHE SAID
THAT HE SAID . . .

Lord Jesus,

Remember that old saying? Something about intelligent people talk about ideas, less intelligent people talk about events, and unintelligent people talk about people.

Well if that's true, the kids at my school have a case of terminal stupidity. The only thing they seem to be able to talk about is each other.

Most of it is so dumb.

"Did you know that she may be pregnant?"

"Did you hear that he's really gay?"

"Didn't you know that he'll be expelled the next time he looks at a teacher the wrong way. I happen to know someone who heard the assistant principal talking to him just the other day."

"I can't believe it but he says that she tried to commit suicide just the other night. Right at home. Her parents stopped her just in time. I know it's true because he told me that she told him herself."

And all like that.

Maybe we've all been together too long. Maybe we know

each other so well that we can't find anything else to talk about anymore.

And maybe we are so bored with each other we have to make up stories because most of what we do from day to day is really too dull.

What really irritates me about it all is that I don't stand up to all of these talkers and tell them off. I ought to just say, "That is a lie! I know it's a lie because I know that person and what you are saying simply isn't true."

But I usually don't. I usually just keep quiet and listen, just like everyone else, even when I know the story isn't true.

And the worst part is, sometimes I find myself believing all of that trash. I find myself thinking less of the person they say is gay or turning away from the guy they say is getting expelled, or avoiding the one who they say OD'd at the party last weekend.

That's so ignorant! How could I do that? Why do I do that? I know these rumors are started by small people who think they're cute or by jealous or angry people who don't know how else to hit back. And I still listen.

Can You help me?

I'd like to have the strength to be the one who kills rumors instead of spreads them. I'd like to be the one who stands up to the talkers and shows them how much hurt their stupid rumors cause. I'd like to be the one who looks for the people who are being run down by the rumors and let them know they still have a friend anyway.

At least then I wouldn't feel so guilty about the rumors that pass through my head and sometimes through my mouth.

But even if I can't stop the rumors, help me ignore what they are saying and look past the words and see the people who might need my help and Yours.

Help me listen only enough to rumors to find the people who might be hurting, so that I can reach out to them with Your love and Your forgiveness.

I'd like that.

Thanks.

ASK . . . SEEK . . . KNOCK:
G, K, R.

ZIP-LOCK MOUTH

Lord Jesus,

One of the neatest new inventions I know about are those little plastic bags with the lock top. All you do is press the two little tracks together and the thing is sealed up tight.

Now I know You knew what you were doing when you created people, but a little addition like that on my mouth would sure have saved me a lot of trouble. I mean if I could just press my lips together in the morning before I go to school, I'd sure be better off, and I know several teachers who would appreciate it too.

My trouble is, I just can't seem to keep quiet.

It's not that I think that I have to answer every question, or even that I have to ask a question in every class. It's more that I think I have to point out teachers'—shortcomings, let's call them—for everyone to hear about.

But it drives me crazy. Why do teachers act like that?

This one guy, I guess he's a teacher because he stands up in front of class. He is always running people down. Now why does he have to do that? He says to poor Al, and everyone knows Al is slow—you'd have to be a complete jerk not to know **103** it—he goes, "My boy, your grades in this class are approaching the worst ever recorded in my grade book." And that right in front of the class. And I think he even thought that was funny or clever or something. Well, anyway, I ended up in the assistant principal's office for what I said to him. But does he have a right to hurt someone just because he's the teacher? I should have just kept my mouth shut like everyone else. But he makes me so mad.

Then there was that time that biology teacher introduced a new grading system. She said something like, "In this class my policy will be to give each person a grade according to his or her ability and how he or she has measured up to what is expected." All of which sounded pretty good, I guess. And I wasn't mad about it or anything. I just wanted to understand what she was talking about.

Still, I would have been better off just to press my lips together and lock them up, but I couldn't. Well it ended up that I said her idea was "stupid" or something worse than that. And it was, for that matter. She hadn't any idea how she was going to work out her crazy system of grades—she was just flapping her mouth. But I was the one who ended up in the office again.

It's not that all the teachers are bad. You know that. I mean some of them are okay. In all, they try to be fair. They know what they are teaching and teach it, and some of them even try to listen to you when you have a problem or question.

And I guess I'm asking a lot when I expect all of them to be at least able to do their job. But it seems to me that if a person doesn't like kids, or doesn't like teaching, or doesn't know how to teach he should do something else—sell insurance or build garages or something. Why does he need to stay in the classroom, do these unbelievable things to kids, and get me in trouble?

I really got in a mess with the principal the other day, You know. But it seemed like a good idea at the time. I mean people who work in factories and all have people to complain to when things aren't going right. I just thought that we ought to have something like that in high school—a place to go and complain when teachers are unfair. Well, the idea got attention. I was warned about my "attitude" again, and I even got a threat of suspension, which was a new low for me.

Can You help me? But I don't even know what kind of help to ask for. I know I gotta stop putting teachers down in front of their classes, even if they are wrong. But does that mean I have to sit quiet for the rest of my life every time I see somone doing something to hurt someone else, every time they are unfair, every time they act like they can use people and treat them like things? Do I have to bite my tongue and zip my mouth and just sit there? Mom says I'll have a lot more peaceful life if I do. Is that what I'm supposed to have, a peaceful life?

But maybe there is a way I could see all those things and do a better job of handling them. I know I could do better with the teachers. If I could just keep from getting mad, and talk to them after class. Maybe they would still tell me to get lost, but they might listen better.

I guess I don't want to ask you to zip up my mouth or help me ignore the bad way people treat each other. But I could use Your help with my temper. Help me control the anger and let it help me do better at dealing with those things that are unfair and unkind and just plain wrong.

I can't seem to ignore them. I guess I don't want to. But forgive me when I act out of pride instead of concern for others. Give me more patience so that what I do will help instead of make the hurt worse for everyone. And help me care about—maybe even love—all teachers, even those who really ought to be out there building garages.

Thanks.

ASK . . . SEEK . . . KNOCK:
J, O, U.

FINALS

Lord Jesus,

The trouble with finals is that they are so final.

I mean, I'm not crazy about any tests. I get pretty nervous when I have to take a test, especially in a subject I'm not too good at. But when it comes to finals I get practically paralyzed. See, I don't understand how anyone expects finals to work anyway. When you think about it, how is it possible to get everything into your head that the teacher thinks you are supposed to have learned in a semester?

I usually start studying for finals by flipping through the textbook, looking over all my notes, reading over all the past tests and then crying for about a half hour. It just looks so impossible.

I'd like to know who invented finals, anyway. I'd like to talk to him about the whole idea. I mean, I can understand tests all right. I know teachers have to find out if you are learning what you are supposed to be learning as you go along. And also they need something to put on your report card. But what is the idea with a final? Is it supposed to find out who has the best memory for lots of little details that you'd probably be better off forgetting anyway?

I always think that some day my brain will get overloaded on facts. I think they are kind of piling up in my head. And somewhere in my brain is this huge dump all filled with dates about the discovery of America and all the names of the little animals in biology and all like that. I don't know what they are all doing up there and I sure don't know what I'm going to do with them all, but I hope I don't get an oversupply and burn out all the circuits.

I guess some people like finals. I guess they can just remember all that stuff and put it on the paper without a problem. For me it seems impossible. The more I go over the text, notes, and tests, the more it all gets muddled up in my head. By the time of the final I'm can't even remember how to spell my name.

I guess I think it's not fair. Why should I have to compete with kids who can remember anything? I mean, there's this guy in history who not only remembers all the dates, he remembers the page you can find them in the textbook. When it comes to the final, I'm lucky if I can remember the name of the course.

My parents talk about college, but I don't think I can do it. Not that I'm stupid or anything like that. I can understand most things when the teacher explains them. But I have such a bad time with finals. And I suppose that in college you have finals about every other week. I'd get burned out by the end of the first month.

I wish You could make me smarter. No—not really smarter, just able to remember better. Or at least less afraid of the finals when they do come.

Can you help me?

I'm not trying to be a great brain, or even get all A's. That's not all that important to me. But I'd like to be able to take a final and feel like it shows what I have learned and not just what I'm not able to keep from forgetting.

I guess I am going to have to take some kind of finals all my life. Help me learn to see the final as a challenge instead of an enemy. Maybe I'd do better then.

I sure couldn't do any worse.

Forgive me for the times I have been angry with You for the troubles I have with finals and other tests, and make me more confident that I can do at least as well as I am able on every test that comes by.

Help me be able to say, "Finals next week," and not get that terrible sick feeling inside.

I'd like that.

Thanks.

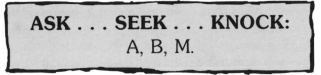

ASK . . . SEEK . . . KNOCK:
A, B, M.

MY NECKLACE

Lord Jesus,

You know, most of the time jewelry is no big deal for me. I guess I like to wear some once in a while, but half the time I can't find it because I left it in the bathroom, or somewhere else.

But there's that one necklace that bothers me. Not that it's so special. I don't think it cost my parents more than about ten dollars. And I don't even remember why they gave it to me. It must have been for a birthday or something.

Don't get me wrong. There's nothing wrong with the necklace. It's kind of pretty—fine gold chain. And the cross is delicate with scroll markings along it. It is basically a very nice piece of jewelry. I guess it's the cross that bothers me.

Funny, but most people ignore it. To most people it's just another piece of decoration to wear around your neck. Oh, sometimes I do I get weird reactions. Like from the guy who laughed at me for wearing it. And then there was that old lady who had to tell me the story of her conversion just because she saw the cross on my necklace. But all of that really isn't so important.

The trouble I have is that I don't always think about the necklace as just another piece of jewelry. Oh, I guess mostly I ignore it too. I just forget it's there at least most of the time. But sometimes, all of a sudden, even before I think, I find myself making sure it's inside my sweater where it can't be seen. And most of the time that happens when I'm doing someting I wish I wasn't.

I guess at those times I feel like I'm letting You down. Like I pretend I'm some kind of a good person, and then I do some stupid thing that I don't really want to do, and right away I know I've made a lie out of the cross I'm wearing. Then I don't want people to see it. I don't want them to know that I call myself a Christian. Because if I was a real Christian I would be doing a better job of showing it to people.

Like the time I lost my temper at Meg. Poor Meg, and all she did was try to be my friend. And there was that other time I copied Steve's answers. The worst part was that everyone else knew I copied them too. Or the time I told the lie to my parents so that I could do what I wanted to do instead of what they thought I should do—and all of those other times like that. Then I didn't feel like I should have been wearing the cross at all. That's when the necklace gives me trouble.

Wouldn't you think it would work the other way? Wouldn't you think it would remind me of who and what I was as Your child and help me stop doing those wrong things? Wouldn't you think it would make me a better person? All it seems to do is make me more ashamed of myself. I still do the bad stuff, I just feel worse about it. And that's why it's easier just to forget the cross and wear some other kind of jewelry. Something that doesn't mark me, or make me think, or make me feel bad.

Can You help me?

I'm not asking You to make me perfect. I know that's not going to happen. But can You help me be more like what You and I expect me to be? Can You help me see the cross I wear as something to be proud of, something that reminds me of Your love for me? And help me remember that it also tells me of Your forgiveness for me when I do mess up—so I don't have to be ashamed.

But maybe even more important, can You help me show
Your love and forgiveness for others so well that they will think

I am wearing Your cross, even when I'm not?
I'd like that.
Thanks.

> ## ASK . . . SEEK . . . KNOCK:
> ### G, O, X.

OOPS!

Lord Jesus,

Maybe I'm exaggerating, but I think something is not connected up right between my head and the rest of me.

The nurse who wrapped my ankle again said I must be "accident prone"—but that's putting it mildly.

Let's face it. I'm just plain clumsy.

I don't think I always was. I mean, when I was younger I seemed to be able to get along without falling on people, tripping over curbs, and dropping the first spoonful of whatever I was eating on the middle of my shirt at every meal.

But since I started to grow, it's like my fingers have turned into frozen stumps, and my feet have started some kind of a war with each other. It's gotten so that the word I seem to use most often is "oops!"

Just this afternoon—I've never been so embarrassed—and I still don't know exactly how it happened. I had to leave band class early for that meeting. And I guess my foot caught on that girl's chair or whatever. Anyway, all of a sudden I was crashing into the trumpet section, and they went over backwards into the trombones—and so on. Well, there are a lot of mad musicians, swollen lips, bent horns, and a deformed music stand to mark my grand exit from band today. Even the sousaphone is turned around the wrong way.

And I don't know what to do about this problem. These fits of clumsiness come on me when I least expect them. I mean, the other day—who else could do it but me? I don't know how it happened, but I fell out of my desk right in the middle of class. Just all of a sudden, crash! And there I was on the floor. The teacher asked if I was ill, you know. Well, I said I slipped. But how could I slip off a perfectly stationary desk seat?

I'm getting pretty tired of this. I mean, I think I ought to wear a sign around my neck that says *Caution! Hanging around me can be hazardous to your health!*

Can You help me?

I don't even know how to ask someone if this is just something I have to live through for a few years or whether I am going to be a walking disaster for the rest of my life.

What an awful thought that is. I can see myself falling over the kneeler at my wedding, or dropping my new wife carrying her over the threshold. Or I might be receiving some important business person at my plush office in some grand office building and suddenly fall over backwards in my chair. And there I'd be with my feet up in the air. I mean, it's too terrible even to think about.

I need Your help. I don't know what else to do. I don't think any doctor has a cure for clumsiness.

I keep telling myself to be more careful, but that doesn't seem to help at all. In fact, sometimes when I'm trying to be most careful I have the most trouble. When I fell in band, you know, I was trying real hard not to step on anyone's feet—and there I went!

Help me learn to live with this awkward body I have. I guess I'll have to learn to do the best I can with it. I'm sure I won't be able to trade it in.

I'm not asking for a miracle that would suddenly make me into a picture of grace and balance. Just help my head and the rest of me get a little more coordinated, so that maybe I can get through a few days at a time without saying "OOPS!" too often.

Can You help me learn to be a little more at home with **113** my hands and feet and all. Maybe we could get this all working together a little better.

I'd like that.

Thanks.

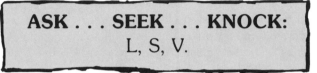

ASK . . . SEEK . . . KNOCK:
L, S, V.

THEY'RE YELLING AGAIN

Lord Jesus,

I don't know which is worse any more, the yelling or the silence.

It's been so long since they got along. I think I remember when they did. Back when I was little. It seems like Mom used to laugh a lot then, and Dad would bring her little gifts or flowers. Maybe I was too young to hear the yelling then. But I can hear it now.

Sometimes I wonder what they can find to fight about all the time. It seems like they fight about everything. Last night they were yelling at each other about the stupid garbage, believe it or not. From my room I couldn't really tell what the whole problem was, but I guess Mom nailed Dad because he ought to help her more around the house—the usual stuff. And he was yelling back. Finally he went out of the house with a big slam of the front door, like he does. Sometimes it seems like he is just looking for a fight so he'll have an excuse to get out of the house again.

I don't really want them to get a divorce, but they are driving each other and me crazy with this fighting all the time.

115

And I don't know what to do for them. I can barely talk to either of them when they're alone, they're so depressed and all. And when they're together—there's no talking—just yelling.

How could it happen? How could that much hurt and hate get built up between two people? Maybe there is something they could have done when they first started to have trouble. But I don't think anyone can do anything now. They don't even talk sense to each other any more.

I don't think they want to give up on each other. They went to talk to the pastor together a couple of times. But that didn't seem to do much good either. I guess they were a little quieter for a while, but that only lasted a few days.

The trouble is that even though I should do my best to ignore this and tell myself that it is their problem—it is really getting to me. Most of the time, but especially when they fight, I feel completely alone. It's like being in a great dark cave where I can hear echos of their words, but I can't reach them, and all I can do is sit in the darkness and shiver from the cold.

And at school. I know I don't listen to the teachers half the time. I guess I spend too much time thinking, or trying not to think. And sometimes I don't even hear my name when a teacher calls on me.

The counselor called me in for a talk. I told him a little bit about the trouble the folks were having, but what can he do? He said I should come in and talk to him whenever I feel like it's getting too much for me—and maybe I will.

I guess, most of all, I'd like to be able to do something for Mom and Dad. They are both really great people, and they could be happy together—at least I think they could. But what can I do now? What can they do now?

In my head I tell myself I wouldn't mind if they got divorced, but I know that really isn't true. I feel so empty and alone when I think about them splitting up. But I hurt for them when I think about them staying together and yelling at each other. I don't jknow which is worse.

They make me so mad I'd like to bang their heads together to see if it might knock some sense into them. And I guess if I thought that running away from home would help, I'd do it. But I don't think even that would wake them up. They'd probably fight over whose fault it was that I ran away.

I guess all I can do now is hang around and pick up the pieces when they do split up. I think it will just about wipe them out.

Can You help me? I'll need a lot of help to get through this. I don't know if I'm strong enough to be the one who gets pulled on by both of them. Can I really stand it if they break up? What if I end up in pieces too—crying and carrying on? And I know that will just make it worse for everyone.

Help me be strong enough to help them. I know they will need me to be, and I don't know if I can do it.

And take care of them both. I love them very much. I don't want to see them hurt any more. I can't reach them. Can You help them? I can only put them in Your care.

And give me the patience not to give up on them and the strength to keep forgiving them.

I know our life together will never be the same as I remember it from when I was little. But help each of us get out of the dark caves of our loneliness and pain, and to love each other again.

I'd like that.

Thanks.

ASK . . . SEEK . . . KNOCK:
P, Q, R.

ASK . . .
SEEK . . .
KNOCK . . .

[Jesus said] Ask, and you will receive; seek, and you will find; knock, and the door will be opened to you

—Matt. 7:7 TEV

A. Read Matt. 6:24-34. Pick out the verse that helps you the most when you are worried. Write the verse on a tablet or book jacket and read it often.

B. Read Psalm 23 and John 10:1-17. Tell someone else how it feels to know that Jesus is your "Good Shepherd."

C. Read Mark 10:13-16. Think about the ways you are a "little child" in your relationship with Jesus.

D. Read John 8:3-11. Write down or share with someone what it means to you that Jesus forgave the woman. When is that forgiveness most important to you?

E. Read Rom. 8:18-27. What help for your prayers do you find?

F. Read 1 Peter 2:9-10. At what times in your life would these verses be most helpful to you? How can you keep them ready for those times?

G. Read Heb. 4:14-16. Write down a temptation that is troubling you right now. Take it to Jesus, knowing that He understands. How does it make you feel to know that you are forgiven?

H. Read Rom. 8:29. How can you share the truth of this passage with someone who is hurt or grieving?

I. Read Matt. 11:28-30. Put Jesus' promise into your own words. Share the promise with someone else.

J. Read Matt. 28:17-20. Write down both the promise and the purpose in the verses. Which is most important to you now?

K. Read Psalm 142. Describe the problem you think the psalmist was going through as he wrote the psalm. How might you put the same thoughts into your own words?

L. Read Rom. 8:31-39. Put the message of the verses into simple words, as if you were explaining them to a child. What might you say? How do the words help you?

M. Read Psalm 145 aloud. Then read it as loud as you can without disturbing the neighbors. When do you feel most like shouting out words like these?

N. Read Luke 23:44-49. Describe the scene (in words or pictures) as completely as you can. Share your description with someone else. How does it make you feel to know that Jesus died for you?

O. Read Phil. 4:4. How can you express your joy? How can you share it with someone else?

P. Read Col. 3:5-17 with your family. Read the verses as though Paul was writing personally to you. What can you do to live out this New Life in your family?

Q. Read 1 Corinthians 13. Substitute the phrase *God's love for me in Jesus* for the word *love* ("charity," KJV) throughout the whole chapter. Why is His love eternal?

R. Read Eph. 3:14-19 as though it were a prayer for you or someone you love. Substitute another's name (or your own) for the word *you* as you read the verses. What can you add to the prayer?

S. Read Luke 15:11-32. Write a letter that the younger son might have sent to a friend after he had returned home. What would he have said about his father? How does it help you to know that the older brother was forgiven too?

T. Read quickly through the Gospel of John. Pick out each place **119**

Jesus says "I am." List the things He compares Himself to. What does each mean to you?

U Read over the commandments in Exodus 20. How does remembering the commandments help you when you are tempted? What commandment is most important to you now?

V. Read Judg. 6:1-16. How does it help you to know that God does not always choose the brightest and the best for His tasks? Why did God choose Gideon? Why does He choose you?

W. Read 1 Peter 1:3-9. Put Peter's words of hope into your own words. How can you share that hope with someone else?

X. Read John 20. Write down or describe the events in chapter as if you had been there. What feelings do you experience as you tell about the first Easter?

Y. Read Psalm 51. How might you put your thoughts in writing as you think of a sin that troubles you? How does it help you to know that God has forgiven you in Jesus?

Z. Read Matt. 26:17-30. Think of what Jesus is giving you as you receive His body and blood in Communion. How can you share that gift with someone else?

God, . . .

Can You still hear me?

Can You help me?

Sometimes it seems like all I do is complain to You. But they won't leave me alone. They keep making fun of me, laughing at me, pointing at me.

I feel so hurt inside. It's like I'm all alone and empty and afraid.

If only I could get away—if I could run or fly away.

Sometimes I dream I'm like a bird. And I just fly so far away they never find me again—so far away I get to a quiet place to rest and You are there to hold me and help me.

I don't know where else to go.

I know You will hear and help me. I know You love me. It doesn't matter how many are against me or how much they

think they can hurt me. You are bigger and better than all of them. Your love is greater than any of my problems. You have touched me, helped me, comforted me so many times in the past.

Because of Jesus I will lean on You, depend on You, keep coming to You. And You won't let me down.

—*Based on Psalm 55*

God, . . .

Sometimes it seems like You're angry with me. Like You are punishing me with all these problems.

I've had it! I'm at the end of my rope! I can't take any more.

Can't You hear me? Can't You help me? What good will I be to You if I'm dead?

I am so tired of complaining, of crying, of feeling sorry for myself. And the problems won't go away. They just pile up one on another.

I need You to help me. Can't the hurting stop?

Help me face these problems and get them down to size so that You and I can handle them together.

I know You will help me. You always have before. I know You will hear me because You have promised.

—*Based on Psalm 6*

God, . . .

I thought You were going to love me and take care of me. Isn't that what You promised? Well, I sure haven't seen much evidence of any help lately.

It seems like half the world hates me and the rest think I'm some kind of a reject. They keep making these comments about how I think I'm some kind of a saint or something. I try to live like You want me to. I try to do what You tell me. I don't make fun of You or use Your name to swear like they all do. I don't join in with them when they run people down, when they break the rules, do drugs and act like fools. And all I get for my effort is more trouble, more rejection and more pain.

Is that the way it's going to be? Is that the kind of life I'm going to have if I try to follow You?

121

That's not what You promised. You promised to take care of me.

I did what You wanted and all I got for my trouble was more hurt than I could handle.

It almost seems like You lied to me.

Can't You help me?

—*Based on Jer. 15:15-18*

God, . . .

I'm too young to die.

Why is this happening?

I can't believe my life is over already. I've barely had time to live.

Why have You done this to me?

They tell me there is nothing anyone can do. I'm going to die and I will never see my friends or family again.

God, I am so afraid. I can't seem to think of anything else. I wake in the morning with a start and a cry. And all day the terrible shadow of death darkens every moment. I find myself shaking like a frightened sparrow and crying like a lonely dove.

God can't You help me?

Can't You end my suffering and stop that terrible thief from stealing my life away?

I promise You I will dedicate my time to You, every hour You give back to me I will fill with Your praise.

I know You will help me as You have done so often in the past.

Haven't You always protected and forgiven me? And surely when I am dead I can neither serve You nor praise You.

Save me, and I will tell the world about Your love and faithfulness and I will spend my life praising You.

—*Based on Hezekiah's "Song": Is. 38:9-20*

God, . . .

Why have You made me like I am? Your Word has captured

me. I speak it, and I am taken for a fool.

Everyone laughs at me and makes jokes about me.

When I say and do what You want me to, they mock me and make fun of me.

I even tried to change. I thought I would ignore You and what You expect of me. I thought I might have some peace that way.

But You set a fire in me, and I cannot keep still. I can't seem to help myself. When they do wrong, I must tell them, show them, cry to them that they have broken Your Law.

But they don't want to hear about that. They just call me names and scorn me. They treat me like I'm a hopeless reject.

I know You will stay with me. I know You will not let them wipe me out.

I turn those who hate You and Your Word over to You. You are the one who will have to judge them.

Meanwhile I will keep on praising You, keep on speaking for You and You will help me. I know You will.

—Based on Jer. 20:7-13

God, . . .

It's so great to know that the sin that has been ruining my life is finally taken away.

It's like getting out from under a great weight.

The whole time I kept the hurt inside me, it was like I was being pulled down into the pits. I felt like you were always pointing Your finger and me. And I was so afraid. It was almost like dying.

Finally, I told you all about it, even though I was so ashamed of what I had done.

And I know You have forgiven me, because I feel new and free again.

In Jesus, You took away my sin, and because of Him I know that I can come to You whenever I do wrong and You will forgive me.

I feel like I am alive again. And I want to sing and shout for joy.

—Based on Ps. 32:1-7, 11

God, . . .

How many times have I prayed to You—praised You?
Still You seem so far away right now.
It's like You can't hear me anymore.

Why are all these people saying these terrible things about me, running me down, insulting me?

I haven't done anything to them. I haven't done anything wrong at all.

I only tried to be friends with them and help them. For my trouble they turn on me and keep attacking me.

Help me and protect me from these ignorant people who are trying to hurt me.

I am so tired, so run down, so sick at heart.

And all because they keep on trying to get me.

I know You love me. Help me and save me. Not for my sake. But let them know that You are the one with power. You are the one who loves and protects His children.

Then I will praise You in front of everyone, even those who thought You had left me alone to suffer their insults.

—Based on Psalm 109

I DON'T WANT TO COMPLAIN, BUT...

by Ted Schroeder

Adolescence can be a wondrous time of change, growth, and discovery, but it can also bring frustration, disappointment, and pain.

The typical adolescent response to the latter is to cry, indulge in self-pity, or complain. But there's another, more positive, response a Christian teen can opt for: to take his or her complaints to Jesus.

I Don't Want To Complain, But . . . speaks to and for teens in their own words about the frustrations of school, parents, self-image, independence, and other timely concerns. Written in the form of conversations with Jesus, each vignette illustrates that no complaint is too trivial to take to the Lord in prayer. As Ted Schroeder points out, "Prayers that present our troubles to God sound a lot like complaints. But He promises to hear and help, even when we complain."

The "Ask, Seek, Knock" section in the back of the book directs concerned teens to the Bible references that offer understanding and encouragement from a teen's best Friend, Jesus.

Ted Schroeder of St. Louis, MO, is the author of *The Art of Playing Second Fiddle.*

CONCORDIA ®
PUBLISHING HOUSE
3558 SOUTH JEFFERSON AVENUE
SAINT LOUIS, MISSOURI 63118-3968

YO
12-2999
ISBN: 0-570-03964-9

0 78777 03964 6